"This is the unbelievable story of the pilgrimage of ten thousand-plus boys from one tribe in Africa as they confront the horrors of Islam and find hope in Jesus. I highly recommend it."

William D. Boyd, Ph.D.
President, College of Biblical Studies
Houston, Texas

"*Lost Boy No More* is a riveting read—simply one of the most moving books I have read in some time. Abraham Nhial and DiAnn Mills have written an amazing contribution to Christian literature. The narrative of the Lost Boys of the Sudan is a tragically overlooked event in Christian history, and, at long last, the truth is known. I pray every single pastor and Christian reads this book with undiverted attention. It will radically affect your worldview and will stifle the incessant whining of comfortable Christianity. The sacrifices of the church in Sudan make our worst days seem benign."

Dr. Ergun Mehmet Caner
Author, *Christian Jihad*
(Gold Medallion winner)
Liberty University, Lynchburg, Virginia

"*Lost Boy No More* tells the powerful story of young men whose homeland has been ransacked and whose families have been destroyed in a genocidal and hate-filled campaign of terror. Theirs is a story that needs to be told and heard. It is a story of a war-torn country and its innocent victims, of perseverance in the face of horrific odds, and of faith in the Lord Jesus Christ. This book lays bare the brutal reality of human suffering that continues to be visited upon millions in the central and southern central regions of Sudan. It is an account that will make you look differently at the world and the plight of those who yearn for liberty."

Dr. Richard Land, President
The Southern Baptist Convention's
Ethics & Religious Liberty Commission

"During every holocaust, every genocide, every ethnic cleansing, the world squeezes its eyes shut and stops its ears. And ever after, it vows 'Never again!' It must not be so with the Body of Christ. *Lost Boy No More* is must-reading for Western Christians. May it open our eyes, bend our knees, and spread our arms wide to embrace our Sudanese brothers and sisters."

Brad Phillips
President, Persecution Project Foundation

"The heartrending stories of *Lost Boy No More* will stay with you for a long time. The boys of the Sudan had their childhood stolen from them and replaced with a nightmare. The stories will also fill you with hope, as they exemplify the resilience of the human spirit."

Congressman Tom Tancredo

LoST BOY
No MORE

LOST BOY
NO MORE

A TRUE STORY
OF SURVIVAL AND SALVATION

Abraham Nhial
and DiAnn Mills

BROADMAN
&HOLMAN
PUBLISHERS

Nashville, Tennessee

0-8054-3186-1

Published by Broadman & Holman Publishers,
Nashville, Tennessee

Dewey Decimal Classification: 962.4
Subject Headings: SURVIVAL \ CHRISTIAN LIFE
                    SUDAN—HISTORY—1983–, CIVIL WAR

Scripture quotations are taken from the Holman Christian Standard
Bible®, Copyright © 1999, 2000, 2002, 2003 by Holman Bible
Publishers.

2 3 4 5 6 7 8 9 10 08 07 06 05 04

*This book is dedicated to
the Lost Boys of Sudan,
their families, friends, and all who
love and support them.*

Contents

Foreword

I first heard about the Lost Boys of Sudan several years ago through news reports. The stories told were almost too unbelievable to be true. I wanted to know more but lost track of the story. Then, DiAnn Mills gave me the honor of reading this book. I was once again captured by what may be one of the saddest and yet greatest stories of our time.

The story of Abraham Nhial and the sixteen thousand boys who wandered Africa for years, alone and afraid, is a story of biblical proportions. People of all religions are familiar with the accounts of Abraham of the Bible. His faith in God led him and his family on a journey that laid the foundation for the world. Few, however, know the story of the modern-day Abraham as told in this incredible book.

DiAnn Mills takes the reader on a heartbreaking and inspiring journey from the Sudan to Ethiopia and Kenya. Sixteen thousand boys came together from all across the Sudan, as they fled from those attacking their villages and killing their parents, brothers, sisters, and other family members. These boys were alone, with only each other to guide the way, provide food, and try to protect each other. In their journey to safety, they had to survive rebel soldiers, crocodiles, and the elements of the unforgiving countryside. Many did not survive.

The Lost Boys eventually found safety in Ethiopia, but it, too, was overrun by rebels and the boys had to go on the run again. Their journey led them back to the land they had fled in fear and then on to a United Nations refugee camp in Kenya. Many ended up, and still live in, the United States, where they are receiving an education and waiting to return to their homeland one day.

This book is more than a story of an incredible journey by brave young boys. It is most importantly a story of faith. This is why I see this work by DiAnn Mills as a story of biblical proportions. The faith of these boys in Jesus as their Savior, despite the ordeals they suffered in their journey and still face today, can be compared to the stories of faith in the Bible. The faith of the Lost Boys is an example to all in the world of the peace, hope, and promise of God's Word. Every believer will be inspired by the story of the Lost Boys. Nonbelievers will understand, possibly for the first time, how faith in Jesus Christ is the only answer for the struggles of this world.

This story is also one of the politics and religion of this world. In a time when the Christian and Islamic faiths are on a collision course in much of the world, DiAnn Mills walks us through each faith so that the reader has a better understanding of the present-day conflicts through the backdrop of her story on Abraham's journey across Africa.

You will be shocked, saddened, inspired, and filled with hope as you read *Lost Boy No More*.

Dan Patrick

Dan Patrick is author of the best-selling book *The Second Most Important Book You Will Ever Read,* a personal challenge to read the Bible. He is owner of Houston Broadcasting and hosts a daily radio talk show. An award-winning veteran of more than thirty-five years in the media, he is a regular contributor to Fox News, MSNBC, and other networks. He is often the guest host on national radio shows for Michael Reagan and Laura Ingraham.

Glossary

AASG: American Anti-Slavery Group

Abid: Slave

ACT: Action by Churches Together

Bilad al-Sudan: Arabic meaning "the land of the blacks"

CCMA: Christian Council of Metropolitan Atlanta

CEAWC: Committee for the Eradication of the Abduction of Women and Children

Condominium rule: When two countries rule a separate country

CPMT: Civilian Protection Monitoring Team

CSI: Christian Solidarity International

CWS: Church World Services

Durra: a type of grain, which is mixed with milk to form a thick doughy porridge

EMM: Episcopal Migration Ministries

ERLC: Ethics and Religious Liberty Commission

Freedom House: A nonprofit organization dedicated to democracy and freedom around the world

GOS: Islamic Government of Sudan, based in Khartoum

GED: General Equivalency Diploma

Ghee: a semiliquid butter made from cows' milk

Human Rights Watch: a humanitarian organization against slave redemption

ICG: International Crisis Group

IGAD: Inter-Governmental Authority on Development, which promotes a social, economic, and scientific community among its members

INS: U.S. Immigration and Naturalization Service

IRC: International Rescue Committee

Jihad: a Muslim holy war against those who do not follow Islamic beliefs

Jubilee Partners: A ministry organization in Georgia dedicated to assisting refugees for the first two months after arriving in the United States

Karkaday: a variety of hibiscus whose flowers are dried, crushed, and boiled into a deep red tea, with sugar added

LWF: Lutheran World Federation

Mujahadeen: Islamic holy warriors

NCC: National Council of Churches

NDA: National Democratic Alliance

NIF: National Islamic Front

NSCC: New Sudan Council of Churches

OLS: Operation Lifeline Sudan. The world's largest humanitarian aid group, made up of UN agencies for assistance to north and south Sudan

Parapoul: a young man between the age of ten and sixteen who is about to enter the rites of manhood in the Dinka tribe. Means "one who has stopped milking."

Qur'an: according to Islam, the sacred text or revelations from God

RRISA: Refugee Resettlement and Immigration Services of Atlanta

SCC: Sudan Council of Churches

Shari'a: the code of law based on the Qur'an

Shirk: blasphemy against Allah

SIM: Sudan Interior Mission

SOAT: Sudan's Organization against Torture

SPA: Sudan Peace Act

SPLA: Sudan People's Liberation Army (founded in 1983 by John Garang), a rebel force of mostly Dinkas striking back at the Muslim forces

SPLM: Sudan People's Liberation Movement, a rebel movement working within southern Sudan to bring about changes by the government that will insure human rights and a better quality of life

SRRA: Sudan Relief and Rehabilitation Association, part of the SPLA

SSFI: South Sudanese Friends International

SSLM: Southern Sudanese Liberation Movement, now a complementary force to SPLM/SPLA (the most widely known rebel movement)

Surah: one of the 114 chapters in the Qur'an

Tamarind: the fruit from a tamarind tree that can be eaten fresh

Tsetse fly: carrier of sleeping sickness

UNHCR: United Nations High Commission for Refugees

Unicef: United Nations International Children's Emergency Fund

Introduction

The first time I heard Abraham Yel Nhial tell the story about the Lost Boys of Sudan, I didn't want to consider such tragedy existed in today's world. I didn't want to believe that children crossed Sudan on foot and faced the perils before them without the aid of parents or adults. I couldn't imagine a civil war lasting two decades. This couldn't have happened. We live in a civilized world.

The more I listened, the more I felt drawn to this proud race of courageous African young men. Curiosity kept me spellbound. How did they survive disease, hostile government soldiers, starvation, and wild animals? I desperately needed to know more. A survivor stood before me, a young man who proclaimed that God had carried him safely through enormous odds.

When first asked to write Abraham's story, I refused. The subject matter was too painful, and I knew I'd shed more tears than write words. But God had a plan, and He wanted the plight of the Lost Boys of Sudan to reach the world. As I talked with Abraham and his story began to unfold, I recognized an incredible faith in God. When I interviewed other Lost Boys, I saw the same intimacy with the Creator. For the first time in my life, I realized how very fortunate I was to live in a country where there is an abundance of food, clothing, shelter, and medical attention. I had no need to fear the government of my country because the officials voted into office care about their people. A deep conviction of selfishness washed over me.

Children are the world's most precious treasure. Most adults will do anything to protect them, but what if children are suddenly forced to fend for themselves in a land beset by civil war? Such is the scenario for the estimated sixteen thousand Lost Boys who began their trek across Sudan—homeless, without the love of parents or family, frightened of the world around them. Each moment was a living nightmare. They struggled to survive and claimed their companions as family with an inexpressible bond stronger than the forces against them. While many made it to safety, others did not. The unfortunate ones died from starvation, disease, wild animals, and enemy forces. Death often looked more appealing than the bleak outlook for the future. These boys held on to a fragile thread of hope—that, by some miracle their lives would be spared.

An estimated two million civilians have given their lives in the civil war, while four to five million more are displaced either in government-controlled camps or in refugee centers outside of Sudan.

Not one single factor caused the civil war; rather, the causes lie in the religion, politics, and economics of the region. The Islamic government of Khartoum has declared a *jihad* (holy war) against southern Sudan. The war's purpose is to force Muslim traditions and practices on all of the people. If this is accomplished, the government will have control of not only the people but also of the valuable resources of the south. The three causes of the civil war are woven tightly into a ball of hatred, with neither side willing to sacrifice its fundamental beliefs in order to establish peace.

The black Africans of the south are spurned by the northern government due to their faith, their ebony-colored skin, and their participation and leadership in the civil war that has raged in varying degrees throughout their land since Sudan became an independent nation in 1956. The south has born the atrocities of the war, as the plight of the Lost Boys depicts.

The journey on which you are about to embark will take you from a pastoral village in southern Sudan to the United States. Abraham expressed his desire for readers to have an overview of what is happening in Sudan, the history of his country, and a deep appreciation for its oppressed people. The problems in Sudan did not develop overnight, and the solutions will take a commitment from all sides to establish a lasting peace. The Lost Boys are the remnant of an oppressed people—a proud people who love their country and dream of a day when their children can live and walk in a free Sudan.

I will never be the same and neither will you.

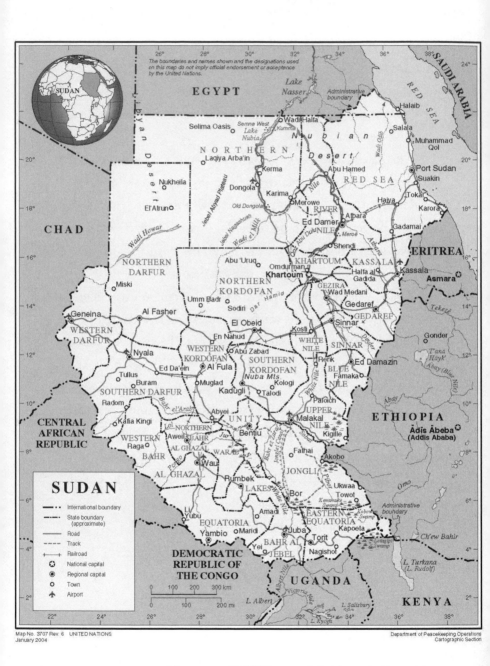

Map courtesy of ReliefWeb, www.reliefweb.int; used with permission.

Sudan Historical Timeline

AD 500   Three Christian kingdoms—
                    Nobatia, Makurra, and Alwa

641   Egypt falls to Arab-Muslim control.

700–1300   Christian faith yields to Muslim penetration.

1504   The Funj rule for three hundred years.
                    Slavery increases.

1820   Ottoman Empire rules Sudan for sixty years.

1881–85   Arab-Muslim rule in Sudan.

1885–95   Sudan famine and disease

1899–1956   British and Egyptian forces take Sudan.
                    Condominium rule

1900s   Slavery ended in Sudan by British mandate.

1922   Egypt gains independence.
                    Britain rules Sudan.

1940   Sudanese nationalism urges independence.

1956   Sudan independent country

1958–69   Government unrest

1969–85   Military control under Jaafar Nimeiri.
                    Civil war increases.

1989   General al-Bashir rules Sudan by force.

1991   SPLA continues civil war.
                    South—famine and disease

1993   Bashir—President

1994   North Sudan escalates civil war. Refugees flee.

1996–Present   Hassan al-Turabi elected president.
                    SPLA continues fighting.

At that time a gift will be brought to the LORD of Hosts from
a people tall and smooth-skinned, a people feared near and far,
a powerful nation with a strange language, whose land is divided by
rivers—to Mount Zion, the place of the name of the LORD of Hosts.

ISAIAH 18:7

Chapter One

Who Are Abraham Nhial and the Lost Boys of Sudan?

If the LORD had not been on our side
when men attacked us,
then they would have swallowed us alive
in their burning anger against us.
Then the waters would have engulfed us;
the torrent would have swept over us;
the raging waters would have swept over us.
Praise the LORD,
who has not let us be ripped apart by their teeth.

PSALM 124:2–6

SOUTH SUDAN 1987. Fear seized nine-year-old Abraham Yel Nhial and held him captive. Paralyzed by the stories his father had told about the murdering soldiers from Khartoum, the capital of his country, Abraham reached deep inside for courage.

The thundering beat of drums from a nearby village warned of danger and echoed terror across the new morning sky. Abraham knew enemy soldiers marched toward the Dinka villages. They came to loot, steal cattle, and carry away women and children as slaves. His mind raced with questions. If only someone would tell him what to do.

"If you hear the drums telling us that the enemy is coming, run," his father had said. "They kill all who get in their way."

But Abraham couldn't bring himself to obey. Had his father gotten the family to safety? What would happen to the village called Geer where he lived with his grandmother? He stood alone in the middle of Nyakrar, the fenced cattle camp, surrounded by the longhorn cattle so precious to his people. Even here, he was a day away from Geer and his beloved grandmother. If he left the cows, he would be neglecting his responsibility. Abraham trembled. He wanted to hide. His heart pounded so hard that he thought it would burst through his chest. He must get back to Wun Lang, his father's village along the Lol River, but that was two days away.

The drums continued. He pressed his palms against his ears in hopes the sound would stop, that the warning meant nothing. If he cried loud enough, his uncle might find him, reassure him that danger had passed. Maybe Abraham's uncle would take him to his father's village to show him the enemy had not brought destruction. When no one answered his pleas, Abraham began to run. His stomach churned at the thought of the enemy taking his father's cows or worse yet, harming his family. He had to see for himself—to see if he could find help. Abraham wrestled with the fear and the desire to take on the role of a man.

He tore through the fenced pen, past the cows, and ran. His legs and sides ached like needles pricking his entire body. Every breath caused his chest to burn. Other villages were closer than Wun Lang, but he denied himself rest or to ask for something to eat. The enemy might be waiting. Instead, he hid during times when his body craved a moment's reprieve. He avoided the thick forests because he'd never been there before, and the dense growth was full of wild animals and poisonous snakes. The tall grasses hid him like a protective coverlet.

When Abraham arrived at Wun Lang, he found the enemy soldiers had left. The smell of burning, thatched-roof huts filled his nostrils and a stench of something he couldn't define but would never forget. Dying embers and gusts of smoke were all that remained of many homes. He stared at the bodies of his relatives and friends: lifeless forms that once laughed, talked, danced, and worked. Now blood flowed from their mutilated bodies. He'd never seen a dead person, for in his village children were not permitted to see a corpse. Never had he viewed a sight so terrible. Fear reigned where he allowed himself to feel at all.

His village had once held a thousand people; now there were none. Horror beyond his worst nightmare appeared before his unresponsive dark eyes. He had no idea what had happened to his parents, four sisters, and two brothers. Their bodies did not lie among the others. Had they escaped the soldiers? Where were they?

Abraham drew in a breath and slowly turned around. The devastation left him in shock and confusion. He wondered again what he should do. His heart longed to stay in the village, to see if anyone returned, but concern for his family and himself forced him to make a decision. He looked to the jungle and began to run again. For two hours he tore through the wilds, sensing the enemy breathed its hot breath at his heels. The cooler air from the canopy of trees masked the dangers lurking as real as the soldiers who had attacked his father's village. Monkeys shrieked. Birds called out as though mocking his fright, and a snake slithered across his path.

Abraham raced on until he caught up with about one hundred boys who had faced the same tragedy. Familiar faces gave him temporary hope. One of them must know where the people from his village hid, where safety and shelter could be found. Then he saw the bewilderment in their eyes—and he knew he wore the same haunted look. This could not be real. What had happened to his peaceful world? Abraham attempted to stop shaking; the urge to cry tore through him. In his heart he realized the pain would be a part of him forever.

Some of the boys were from Abraham's village and others came from neighboring communities. He caught sight of his older cousin Yai, a tall, slim, handsome boy. Relief consoled Abraham for a moment. But the lines on his cousin's young face and the agony in his voice spoke of a chasm too wide to bridge.

"I went back to my father's village." Abraham swiped at the tears flooding his eyes. "So many bodies."

Yai and Abraham embraced. Words could not express the grief piercing their hearts. All they could do was cling to each other and cry.

"I couldn't find my parents or my brothers or sisters," Abraham said. "Do you know where they are?"

"I haven't seen them. Did you see any of my relatives?"

Abraham held his breath. "I saw your uncle among the bodies."

Yai glanced away then back to Abraham. "I don't think we will ever find our families."

The Islamic government of Sudan (GOS), based in the north, had used ground forces and air raids to attack the villages of southern Sudan. Soldiers had riddled adults and children with bullets, although some of the younger children, especially the girls, were taken as slaves. Nearly all of the boys were in the fields watching their cattle, sheep, and goats when the troops attacked. Other northern strikes alerted the people with the sound of gunfire, the death-whistle of bombs splitting the air, or the beating of drums signaling impending danger. Many were just rising to meet the dawn of a new day when the enemy opened fire.

When the sound of bloodcurdling screams echoed in the boys' ears, they ran until exhaustion forced them to stop. They were the lucky ones, able to outrun the soldiers who pressed into the villages. The boys hid until they felt certain the soldiers had not followed them or didn't lurk in the tall grass. The boys crept from behind brush, rock, and trees with the gruesome image of their murdered families and friends forever embedded in their minds. The boys hoped to find others who escaped the decimation, anyone who would offer comfort and reassurance that the tragedy had ended.

The day wore on, and the torrid sun began its slow descent across the African sky. But with dusk approaching, Abraham and his new brothers had additional fears, for dangerous animals stalked the evening shadows. The boys built fires from wood or dried cow dung and huddled around the light and warmth. They listened to the roars of prowling predators and wondered which one of them would be the next victim. For some of the boys, it didn't matter; their spirits had died with their families. They had become the Lost Boys of Sudan.

Abraham walked with Yai on their journey to find safety. Eventually the two walked together all the way to Ethiopia. Among the boys were five eleven-year-olds. They were the elders, the leaders, and Yai was one of them. They led and organized the band of boys in order to keep them together. They were family now, brothers united to find lost families and the peaceful existence they had left behind. The boys looked to the elders for guidance and direction, to find food, and to keep them safe from wild animals and enemy soldiers. Abraham was so grateful that Yai helped lead the boys; he felt safer, as though all their problems and troubles would one day disappear.

Several days passed. They met up with other boys who had experienced the same tragedy—so many tears, so much sorrow.

Most of the boys were barefoot, but Abraham wore sandal-like shoes until they wore out. The rough terrain contained thorns that bloodied their feet and slowed them down.

"There were different kinds of thorns that pierced your feet," Abraham says. "Some went deep and hurt so bad. They were hard to remove. If we were in a dangerous place, we couldn't stop to take them out even in the daytime."

The boys pulled and cut out the thorns the best they could with other thorns. No one had soothing balms or bandages, and the footprints left a trail of blood on the path behind them—a perfect lure for hungry lions.

Exhaustion tugged at their weary bodies. "The elders urged

the boys to keep walking even when they were tired, hurt, and crying," Abraham says. "At times the elders slapped the younger boys or poured water on them—when they had ample water—not to bully them but to help keep them alive.

"Sometimes I wanted to give up. I cried when my feet hurt, when I wanted to sleep or rest from walking so long. It was hard when it rained on us because we had no raincoats or a house to give us shelter. The elders cried too. They felt the same way we did, and they cried for the younger boys who had an even harder time."

"We're not going far, just right over there," Yai would point. "It will take only an hour or so. There we will find help." He sounded confident, so Abraham followed and obeyed.

Abraham and his brothers were afraid to return to their homes, fearful of what they'd find and who might find them. Hundreds of boys became thousands.

He plodded on with his brothers in a southeasterly direction, across the agriculturally rich earth, through the tall, thick grasses, and past the forests of acacia, hashab, talh, and heglig trees. They shared the land with lions, leopards, giraffes, monkeys, elephants, and hyenas. The rivers boasted of crocodiles and hippopotamuses. Tropical birds with their colorful plumage chatted and sang.

Abraham ate mangoes, bananas, and nuts when available. When conditions worsened and food and water were not available, he ate mud. He ate strange, wild plants, which often made him ill with diarrhea or painful sores in his mouth. Rotting zebras or gazelles became an opportunity to fill his hungry stomach.

Abraham wondered about his father. Had he been killed? So many times, he stared at the path ahead and imagined his father coming to get him. He remembered his father had told him their people had been fighting the north for a long time. The men of the north were evil.

"The government of Sudan wants to scare the people living in the south so we will know that they are in control," his father had said. "The Islamic government doesn't like us because we're not Muslim. We refuse to be Muslim."

When Abraham saw the soldiers' light skin, so different from his own, he perceived them as the enemy, as his father described.

As the days passed, Abraham's thoughts changed from those of a selfish child to one who began to think about spiritual matters. He contemplated the things his father had said about the god Nhialic—creator god. According to his father, if a person lived a bad life, he must live and die again.

"What happens to us when we live a good life?" Abraham had asked his father.

"I don't know," his father said. "No one knows."

Abraham pondered his father's explanation. If he did not please Nhialic, would these same terrible things happen again? The practices of his father's worship included sacrificing a white animal for war, family strife, sickness, and forgiveness of offenses. Should Abraham take this religion seriously? He remembered a few Christians who lived in Wun Lang. Did they have any answers for him? But he didn't ask. Abraham was too sad and miserable. Was death only the end of life?

Weeks passed with the encouragement of Yai and the other elders who always said their destination lay just beyond. The elders stationed themselves in front of the brothers, the middle, and rear. Others watched out for the younger ones. Always the elders alerted the boys to dangerous animals. When the brothers could not take another step, the elders carried them. Abraham was too young to carry another boy, but he urged them on. The elders also found whatever food they could, sometimes only grass, leaves, and tree roots. They rationed these so all would have something to eat.

Each new morning the boys plodded ahead, one foot in front of the other, doing what they had to do to stay alive. For life beckoned them to follow and death lurked behind. Abraham strived to ignore the insatiable hunger and thirst. He learned to drink his own urine so he would not die of thirst. Abraham leaned on Yai to help fight the incredible odds against survival. He gave up on ever seeing his family again. Too often the truth shook his dreams and plunged him into reality; he was lost and alone just like Yai and the newfound brothers.

They were attacked by enemy soldiers and lost more of the brothers. They met up with the Sudan People's Liberation Army (SPLA), but the soldiers were unable to help much because of the army's own dire circumstances.

The threat of lions plagued Abraham's life. When the huge animals approached, Yai and the other elders forced the brothers to huddle together in a group with the youngest ones in the middle. At times fright overtook a boy, and he broke out to run despite the elders' attempts to stop him. A lone boy was easy prey to a hungry lion.

"Don't run. Stay together," Yai said. "Be strong. Do not let the lion see you're afraid."

Abraham heard these words so many times that the elders' voices shook his waking and sleeping hours. "The first time we fought lions, I was afraid the elders couldn't protect us. I thought they would run away and leave us alone. I hoped and dreamed my father might come and save us."

The boys used whatever they could find to protect themselves from the lions. The elders instructed them to make lots of noise. Their screams of panic became a shield of defense. If other groups were close by, they helped. The lions moved toward the brothers, closing the gap. The huge, hungry animals roared and tossed their heads.

"We are going to war," Yai told Abraham. Like the loved ones left behind, Abraham understood the brothers had a small chance of survival.

The elders shouted and repeated the same instructions as the lions circled closer. "Don't be afraid. Be brave. If you cry, they will know you are weak and come after you."

Abraham crouched low on shaking legs with the others. Standing made it easy for the lion to leap and knock them down. The boys held weapons, usually big sticks. Abraham knew they would fight a terrible battle. The hot sun beat down hard. Sweat poured over his face and stung his eyes. He swallowed his tears. Brave, he must be brave. All the while, the lions roared. The sound exploded in his ears and intensified the terror crashing around him.

Don't run. Stay together. Be strong. Do not let the lion see you're afraid. Do not be afraid. Be brave.

While the words rang through Abraham's mind, he could not stop the panic raging through his body. He feared for his life and his brothers. Sometimes the boys succeeded in killing the lion or chasing it away. Too often Abraham watched in horror while a lion dragged away one of his brothers—screaming in pain and begging for help. The cries wrenched at his stomach; his heart hammered against his chest. He didn't want to watch the blood, the gore. After all, he could be the next victim.

Abraham pauses in telling his story and swallows hard, the memories too painful to not give reverence to the many who had died. Names and faces from the past creep across his mind. Tears fill his eyes.

"For many years I dreamed that we were being attacked by lions, and there were no elders to protect me. I cried aloud in my sleep. This nightmare doesn't happen anymore, but I still have others."

Hyenas also trailed the boys. These animals were smaller and easier to kill, but still the boys had to conceal their fright when facing these dangerous animals.

Why have I been spared? Abraham asked himself each time he escaped death. *Will I be next?* He tried not to think about what he left behind and the future looked just as foreboding.

His legs ached from walking, and he dreamed of stopping long enough to sleep, filling his empty belly, and drinking until he thirsted no more. He didn't think they would ever reach their destination, if they really had one at all. They passed villages that Abraham didn't recognize, many like he'd left behind. He continued to wonder where they were going. At times he wanted to go back, but he couldn't do that by himself. They had no food, no water, only the constant dread of wild animals and enemy soldiers. Hunger, thirst, fear, and an aching body became a way of life.

Abraham had to obey the elders. He wanted to say, "I will not listen to you. You are not my father." He had to adapt to what

was happening around him or he would die, and most times he
wanted to live.

While Abraham walked, he talked with his new brothers. He
found they all shared in the same disaster.

"What happened when the soldiers came to your village?"
Abraham asked.

"When the bombing began, I ran with the others. I didn't
know where my family had gone, but I kept running. I was six
years old."

Abraham walked on. He asked other boys how the enemy
had attacked their villages.

"The Arab soldiers from the north fired their guns into the
village and burned our homes and shot many people. I hid in the
bush until men from my village found me. It was not safe then.
Later we were separated. That is how I found more boys."

Another brother said, "I saw my friends shot by Muslim soldiers. I ran back to my village, but no one was there. Everyone
ran from the soldiers."

Still another recalled, "I was too small to remember my age.
I was with my cousin. Later they told me I was five and he was
nine."

The accountings all seemed to be the same. "I was four years
old when the Arabs attacked our village. I saw the dead bodies.
The others made me run because we were Christian."

Christian? Did the enemy hate some of the people more than
others? Abraham longed for answers.

Abraham's eyes hold the reality of the boys' bleak existence
then. "We were not used to all of these deaths. And we saw each
other die—in all of the different ways. We had to bury our own

brothers." He pauses, his turmoil too obvious to hide. "This was something new for me—for all of us. It caused great depression. We didn't know what to say or do. We didn't understand. Many of the brothers were so depressed that they couldn't survive physical sickness."

He recalls how other boys expressed their grief.

"Your life has totally changed and now it becomes a matter of survival in a jungle, searching for a new place to stay. You cannot see your family and relatives anymore. You are trying to look for a safer place, but there is no safer place than a jungle filled with wild animals.

"I had to keep walking. I didn't want to die."

William Deng, who now lives in Houston, also tells of his personal struggles. "I remember the water I drank in the desert on our way. It was very bitter water squeezed out of an antelope's intestines. During that journey, some died of thirst and starvation. It was a long journey through hell."

The nightmarish life continued for Abraham and his brothers until they reached a huge river separating Sudan from Ethiopia. This was the river Gilo. After drinking their fill, a few of the boys chose to swim to the other side. Only the strong swimmers escaped the strong currents and hungry crocodiles and made it safely to the opposite bank. The boys pleaded with the Ethiopians to help transport the remaining thousands of boys across the river, and through the use of boats, the boys found refuge within the interior of that country. For Abraham, the journey took four months.

When he reflects on those months, he remembers one triumph. "Most victorious is the friendship and love we had during this journey, and I believe this kind of unity is from God." But one of the questions piercing his heart and mind surrounded the culture of his people, the Dinka tribe. He wanted life as he knew it, and he refused to forget the Dinka ways.

To understand the journey of the Lost Boys, you have to understand where we, the brothers, came from.

ABRAHAM NHIAL

Chapter Two
Dinka Life and Culture

In quiet moments during refugee life in Ethiopia, Abraham considered his Dinka heritage and the traditions of his people. He hoped the soldiers stopped their killing so he could return to his treasured life.

In the northeastern part of the African continent lies Sudan, the largest country in Africa. Sudan's climate varies from blazing deserts to lush rainfall. This vast area contains approximately one million square miles; its size compares to the eastern United States from the Mississippi River to Maine. Sudan borders on Egypt, Eritrea, Ethiopia, Kenya, Uganda, Congo, Central African Republic, Chad, and Libya, and its inhabitants are of Arab descent in the north and the black African race in the south. Through the Sudan flows the great Nile River, the longest river in the world. This country is home to thirty million people. Approximately fifty-six racial and culturally different groups in

Sudan encompass nearly six hundred tribes. Among these tribes more than four hundred distinct languages are spoken.

Southern Sudan is the home of the Dinka, Nuer, Shilluk, and other black African tribes that migrated to the area of Bahr al-Ghazal somewhere around the tenth century. Prior to this time, information about these people was documented through oral history. Arab invaders named the area of North Africa, which is now modern Sudan, *Bilad al-Sudan,* "the land of the Blacks." At that time, this included all the land south of the Sahara Desert.

Several tribes make up the people of southern Sudan: The majority of those affected in the south are the Dinkas, the largest tribe in Sudan. The Dinkas, Nuers, and Shilluks make up the Nilotic tribes who live along the Nile River or in the Nile Valley. In the west are the Azande, Bor, and Jo Luo tribes, and in the far south are the Acholi and Lotuhu tribes, as well as many others.

Most of the Lost Boys are members of the Dinka tribe. These black-skinned inhabitants with squared shoulders and almond-shaped eyes are peaceful cattle owners strongly tied to their families and their Christian beliefs. They live along the White Nile River and westward, thriving in small villages. These people are among the tallest in the world, and their skin is so black that it fairly glistens. They are a slender, graceful people, reminding an observer of royalty. The Dinkas are known as a race of beauty, a hallmark of dignity, and exemplary pride in their traditions and values.

"Some people believe the Garden of Eden was located between the White and Blue Nile." Pride radiates from Abraham's dark eyes. "I'd like to think so too."

Abraham came from the province of Bahr al-Ghazal, Aweil east county, Aweil District, in a village called Wun Lang. This province in the northern section of southern Sudan is the home of the Dinkas. Although Dinkas were not the only tribe represented in the exodus of boys fleeing Sudan, they accounted for the majority of the Lost Boys.

When Muslim soldiers destroyed Abraham's and his brothers' homes and killed their families and friends, the enemy shattered the fundamental values and traditions vital to the Dinka way of life—a culture that has existed for hundreds of years.

Southern Sudan is home to lions, leopards, zebras, gazelles, monkeys, hyenas, antelope, and elephants. Along the shores of the mighty Nile and other rivers live crocodiles and hippopotamuses with a host of waterfowl: herons, black ibises, storks, pelicans, and hornbills. Grasses grow nearly eight feet tall and provide rich feeding ground for the animals. Tropical jungles with towering trees shelter the wildlife that live beneath an assortment of trees. Monkeys chatter, colorful tropical birds sing their songs, snakes slither over the ground cover and around trees, and insects scurry about tending to their life's work.

The Dinkas represent about 10 percent of the population of Sudan, and they are divided into approximately five large groups. Since the earliest accountings of the Dinkas, which date back to the tenth century, the people have herded cattle, sheep, and goats. They live in small tribes, each utilizing enough land to feed and water their animals. The people harvest maize, okra, groundnuts, sesame, pumpkins, and durra, a type of grain used to make thick porridge mixed with milk. The Dinkas eat wild fruit and nuts, depending on the season. The tamarind tree produces brown, lemon-flavored edible pods with a pulp that's sometimes mixed with water for a drink. Large plantations grow karkaday, a type of

hibiscus from which a red, tea-like beverage is made. The fruits
of the shea butter tree, sweet and yellow nuts from the thou tree,
and mangoes all supplement their diet.

Abraham smiles, remembering how the Dinkas pride themselves in personal adornment. They wear jewelry made of brass
and ivory, and they paint their bodies in bright, vivid colors.
Their lifestyle is much the same as it was hundreds of years ago.
The importance of cattle, the role each tribal member plays, traditional beliefs, and rituals are a valued part of the Dinka culture.

Their livelihood depends on longhorn cattle, which serve as
the center of their customs and their measure of wealth. Their
days revolve around the constant quest to find sufficient water
and pasture for the animals. Cattle herders seek flat land to graze
their animals instead of the forests where the tsetse fly breeds,
which carries the deadly sleeping sickness.

In addition to milk, ghee and butter are used as food. *Ghee* is
a by-product of butter-making. The milk by-product is cooked
until it looks like tiny lumps of brown sugar, similar to yeast. It's
placed on top of grain meal or porridge with milk and sugar. This
is a tasty treat for many Dinkas.

"One of the things I miss from my country is ghee," says
William Deng. "The best way I can describe this is that it is like
a fat. Nothing here in America compares to it. It's not just the
taste I miss, but the scent of animals and everything that has to
do with Dinka culture."

Cattle contribute to a host of other uses. Urine is used for
washing and to dye hair; it turns hair orange. The people gather
dung to fuel their fires, and they also claim the ashes repel mos-
quitoes. These ashes are also used as body paint and to clean

teeth. They are rubbed over the cattle to cleanse them and keep away blood-sucking ticks. The cattle are not used for food unless the animal dies. Upon the animal's death, the hide is tanned and used for mats and stretched over drums. In addition, belts, ropes, and halters are made. The horns and bones have a wide variety of useful purposes within the tribal community. Dances, songs, and stories about the valued cattle share an important part of ceremony and tradition. The cows are given a specially chosen name, and some herders will even take on the name of a favored animal.

Every family member is responsible for something that has to do with the cattle. Many Lost Boys feel their culture is lost without these animals. Even peace cannot restore that part of their lives until cattle once again graze in the fertile lands.

During the rainy season, from April to November, the people live in thatched-roof huts walled with mud. Each family needs a number of living areas or huts: one for the parents, a separate hut for boys, a hut for the girls, and a hut used as a kitchen. A large hut is built to house fifty to sixty cows.

Angelo Wol, another brother who misses his culture, says, "I was born in the village of Makuac Pangoung near Gogrial. I was the oldest of three—two sisters and one brother—and my mother taught me to watch out for them. Another job I had was to take care of my father's cattle, sheep, and goats. One of my best memories of living in my village was dancing. I started learning to dance by the time I was four or five years old. I remember it was great fun. One of the most important things I learned at home was the importance of respect. I've never forgotten it. I had to leave my home at the age of seven."

In the dry season, from December until nearly April, all but the ill, aged, and nursing mothers move to the riverbanks where they live until the rains force them back to their permanent homes. Once the rain begins, the grassy areas become a swamp, and the cattle cannot be kept near that area because of the danger of hoof disease. When on the move, the women balance all of their belongings on their heads while the men carry spears and clubs to protect their families, cattle, and possessions.

In the rainy season, showers fall every day in the afternoon. Some areas flood and become impassable, but the people know where the low-lying spots are located and take precautions. Abraham remembers using boats and swimming to combat high water.

The Dinkas hold to the tradition of a chief, who is usually a member of a respected lineage. He listens to the people's complaints and helps resolve disputes in an informal, open-air meeting place. This is often held with elders of the tribe. The chief is not a ruler but a highly esteemed member and honored for his position. The Sudanese government has attempted to appoint those whom they approve of to take on the role of a chief, but those efforts have failed.

The family is an intricate part of the Dinka way of life. They believe family is everything; without it one is nothing. The tribe shares a common ancestral lineage through the father's line. This ancestral lineage links the past to the present, and each member memorizes the common ancestor. This blood kinship, through the males, strengthens the support system of the family or clan. The closer an individual is to the ancestor, the more assistance that person receives from the family in time of need.

Smaller family groups share a direct relationship. These smaller family units share a common cooking fire and help sustain each member. Abraham tells of the importance of family in his village. When a mother gives birth and she has a child age two or younger, the older child goes to live with the grandmother. This is an acceptable part of the Dinka culture. Abraham visited his parents and loved them, but his grandmother always held a special spot in his heart. At the age of five, Abraham began helping with the cows.

In the event there are no sons and the family cannot show a link from the past to the present for the future, the Dinkas have a practice to ensure the protection of the lineage and an heir. If a boy dies, a brother or a close relative takes a wife, and the children born carry the deceased boy's name. Also, if a man dies and has not produced offspring, the nearest relative will marry the wife, and all the children will have the deceased man's name.

When a boy is born he is given his own name, then his father's name, his grandfather's name, and so on. Thus the history of the clan is preserved.

"My name is Abraham Yel Nhial. Yel means 'outside the home' and Nhial means 'the sky.' My father's name is Nhial Yel. His mother's name was Ayak.

Another Lost Boy explains his background. "My full name is Petro Maduk Deng Chol. I was born on December 21, 1979, in a small village called Duk-Payuel in the northern part of Jungulei Bor province in southern Sudan. According to our tradition, when a child is born in this place (Duk) and the family wants to take the name of the place, 'ma' is added to 'duk' and the name becomes 'Maduk,' and this identifies you as a male. But if you are a female, just an 'a' is added to 'duk' and the name becomes 'Aduk.' My last name is Deng Chol. Deng means 'rain' and Chol means 'replacement for the death of a previous child.' My Christian name is Petro; I received it from the church when I was baptized.

"My parents were farmers who dedicated their lives to breeding and raising animals, growing crops, and working in other agriculturally related activities. My dad had five wives and has about thirty children; twenty-five are alive. According to our tradition, history, and culture, it doesn't matter if you marry many women. It is acceptable to be involved in any kind of matrimonial relationship as far as it is legal and one has the wealth to pay for a second wife. My dad and my mother have ten kids, six boys and four girls; I am the second-oldest one."

The Dinka family welcomes the birth of a girl, although she does not contribute to her father's lineage. According to tradition, the bridegroom gives cattle, as many as a hundred, to the bride's family in exchange for his wife. This dowry extends the wealth of the girl's family. The dowry negotiations often involve the extended family of the potential bride and the extended family of the interested young warrior. Once an agreement has been made, the preparations and wedding ceremony focus on much celebration with singing, dancing, and feasting.

The mark of a boy who has undergone the rite of manhood is mutilation. This initiation process is conducted between the ages of ten and sixteen years old. He is called a *parapoul,* which means "one who has stopped milking." The boy will no longer participate in milking, tethering cattle, or gathering dung; he has come of age. His forehead is marked with a series of V-shaped lines that indicate his tribe. The youths are now warriors who guard and protect the village from wild animals and from those who threaten the safety and well-being of the tribe. The young warriors either stay with the cattle all year or only during the wet season. Many are needed during the wet season to plant crops, but their primary role is warrior-protector.

The boys are initiated during harvest time. The evening prior to the markings, their heads are shaved and they gather to sing songs about their clan. At the following dawn, parents escort their sons to the ritual. They sit in a row, cross-legged with their backs to the east. After a blessing, each of the boys takes a turn reciting the names of his ancestors while the man performing the rite grasps the boy's head and makes the appropriate markings. These slashes are deep, but the boy simply stares ahead and continues listing his ancestral lineage. To show pain would bring dishonor to his family and display a lack of courage. The boy is now a man. He will put aside his childish tasks and take on the responsibilities and privileges of a warrior. When the ritual is completed, the fathers wipe the blood from the boys' faces and eyes, then wrap a large durra leaf around the cuts. This will be removed in about a month to reveal the tribal markings. The boys are now permitted to court and marry. In addition, they are given a club, shield, and spear.

The joyous celebration continues with singing and dancing for days to come. The new warrior is also given a young ox, called his "song oxen." This animal is now the youth's most valued earthly possession, and he will dote on it even to the point of training its horns to grow into unusual shapes. Often, the young warrior will take his song oxen with him when he goes courting.

"Most all of the Lost Brothers did not go through the manhood rites. We were too young," Abraham says. "The elders took on the roles as warriors and protectors without the distinction."

In more modern times, the initiation into manhood has taken a drastic change. The parapoul has traveled to the city to earn money to purchase cattle for the bride-price, thus breaking tradition. This practice has led to discontent among the different clans. Still, many of the boys value the initiation process, and the girls prefer the looks of a young man who holds the scars of a Dinka warrior.

The following is the story of Abraham Atem Akech, a Lost Boy who was chosen to enter the United States through the refugee program but left his wife in Kakuma, Kenya.

"My wife and I have known each other since we were very small children. We chose each other from childhood until our marriage in 2001. I have paid thirty-eight cows as bride-price for the marriage to my lovely wife. My father paid them for me since I did not have cattle, and in Dinka culture you cannot take a wife without paying the bride-price.

"I admire her with my whole heart and my love is totally devoted to her. I am sure God has given her to me as my blessing wife no matter what separation we are in now. She is in Kakuma with our little daughter, and I am here in the United States. It is just distance and days, but in God's name I hope we will be together again. Amen."

With the rise of refugee camps resulting from the civil war, the dowry has become increasingly difficult to fulfill. Many Dinka families no longer have cows or have been forced to abandon their land to flee enemy soldiers. The cattle have been sold, slaughtered for food, stolen, killed by northern soldiers, or have died due to the drought. Although the dowry has dropped to thirty or forty cows, many of the men are still unable to pay the bride-price.

The families realize they cannot stop their daughters from marrying. As a result, some marriages are taking place with a promise by the bridegroom to deliver the dowry once the war is over and they can return to their homes. This is an unfortunate position for a people who once held the distinction as Sudan's wealthiest tribe.

Peter Malou, also a Lost Boy, explains more about the Dinka marriage traditions. "Among the Dinkas, a married man cannot stop his wife from being taken by his in-laws because he has failed to pay thirty head of cattle, the minimum bride-price. Therefore, the pregnancy and sneaking away with a girl has increased among young people. When the bride-price is not paid, the parents take their daughter along with any children to work for them instead of allowing her to work for the poor man who is not able to pay the dowry."

Another breakdown of traditional Dinka values is role reversal for men. Because of severe hardships of a country besieged by civil war and starvation, men must now tend to such chores as fetching water and planting gardens. Some of the people have resorted to digging up anthills to find precious grain stored within the mounds.

The old songs and dances depicting the proud Dinkas have been replaced by those of sadness. Some of the Dinkas who follow the Christian faith believe God is punishing them for the high honor they have placed on their animals.

Disease has swept through the land, ending the lives of many men, women, and children. One of the problems is the Guinea worm disease, a serious problem for all of Africa. This is contracted through standing water that has the larvae of the Guinea worm. Once the worm is inside the human body, it can grow to be as long as three feet. It generally takes about a year's time for the worm to make its way to the surface by means of a burning-type blister, usually on the leg. To obtain relief from this, the infected person seeks water where the blister bursts. Then the worm releases more larvae to infect others. The Guinea worm often causes long-term crippling and other side affects. Through the work of Unicef, the World Health Organization, and the Carter Center, founded by former President Jimmy Carter, people in these countries are being educated on how to prevent the disease.

Abraham shares the misery of his people in his eyes. Life expectancy for the Sudanese as of 2001 is age fifty-seven, quite a contrast to those living in the Western world. Abraham preaches that faith in God is the only way for the Sudanese to restore their dignity and self-worth. These people are homesick for their homeland. For many, the war has destroyed their self-confidence. The main difference is the south is fighting a defensive war for its survival, whereas the north's war is one of conquest. The Dinkas and other displaced Sudanese long for a free southern Sudan where the people have freedom of worship without threat of persecution.

He gives strength to the weary
and strengthens the powerless.
Youths may faint and grow weary,
and young men stumble and fall,
but those who trust in the LORD
will renew their strength;
they will soar on wings like eagles;
they will run and not grow weary;
they will walk and not faint.

ISAIAH 40:29–31

Chapter Three

The Endless Journey

William Deng Deng, a Lost Boy who now lives in Seattle, Washington, was born in Marialbai-Awiel in south Sudan on January 1, 1977. His father was a farmer and a cattle keeper. William was brought up by loving parents. When he was five years old, war broke out in Sudan.

"The worst thing happened when our village was attacked by the Islamic fundamentalist government from the northern part of the country. It was early morning when I saw numerous soldiers running in a zigzag way. Within a second, I heard a gunshot like thunderstorm and lightning from here and there. My heart beat so fast that I thought it would burst open. I was truly confused and cried, but no sound or tear came in my eye. I was shocked; I didn't know the direction I took. I ran like a mad person.

"We ran into the beautiful jungle forest of Bahr al-Ghazal with my parents. We slept in the forest at night. The bush was as silent as a grave. We counted the stars in the sky till morning. We forgot sleep that night. We were bombarded from the air and from soldiers shooting. Somehow I got separated from my parents without having time to say good-bye. Great devastation happened on the land. Soldiers set fire to houses, churches, hospitals, and products. So many people lost their lives. I left with a painful and sad heart.

"I fled toward the east to Ethiopia. On the journey, we faced numerous hardships. Our feet were badly blistered. Food was very scarce. Our food was leaves of trees. Hunger, starvation, sleeplessness, and thirst weakened us. We couldn't forget that situation. Our lips were dried as if we hadn't drunk water for a decade, and our bodies were skeletons, all the bones sticking out. Only our teeth identified us. There were many wild preying animals: hyenas, lions, and tigers tried to feed on us. Flesh-eating birds followed us through Ethiopia. Also snake bites and scorpions killed a number of people. It took us almost six months to reach our destination.

"I still remember the horrible war in Ethiopia that killed many people. Some were lost in the jungle forest of Ethiopia. It was a desperate situation in 1991 when we were constantly chased by Ethiopian troops. While we were fleeing from Ethiopian troops, we had to make a very difficult crossing of the Gilo River against a strong current. There were hungry crocodiles and gunfire from Ethiopian soldiers. Some people made a quick crossing by holding on to a rope tied from one side of the river to the other side, and it helped those who did not swim. We were crying out for help. By the help of God some of us crossed the river. The river was about twenty yards across. Twenty thousand people had started the trek, but more than two thousand were lost in the river and forest.

"We settled in two camps, Pochalla and Pakok. There was terrible starvation. No food for almost six months. We ate any trees leaves, roots, and unripe fruits. It didn't matter whether we knew the name of trees or not. We tasted every tree whether it was bitter or not. We ate it even though it was bitter as quinine. If it didn't kill us, we ate it as a food. Those trees saved our lives from the grave.

"We came to Kakuma, Kenya, in 1992 with only sixteen thousand lost boys surviving."

In 1987 when Abraham and his thirty-five thousand Sudanese brothers arrived in Ethiopia, the country was not equipped to take care of so many refugees.

"The small amount of food rationed to us wasn't enough to give life to the thousands of malnourished bodies," Abraham says. "I saw many of the brothers grow weaker and more susceptible to disease, especially typhoid, malaria, whooping cough, measles, and dysentery."

Without the aid of adult parental or guardian care, doctors, or medicine, Abraham watched many more perish. "All we had was each other. And since all of us were suffering either because of weakened bodies or hurting minds—or both—we didn't know how to help each other."

Abraham believed he and his brothers had been forsaken to
suffer in a land not their own. "Many more of the brothers died,
but I don't know how many."

A few months later, the United Nations took note of the dire
circumstances and sent relief workers with food, clothing, medical
supplies, and other desperately needed provisions. The Ethiopians
also provided food, good security, and schooling.

"We were divided into three camps: Dimma, Itang, and
Panyadou," Abraham says. "I wasn't afraid because I knew there
were too many of us to live in one camp. The United Nations
assigned me to Dimma camp, but some of the brothers said the
other camps were better. I didn't care. I was too tired and weak to
walk to another place. In Dimma two Sudanese doctors, Dr. Atem
Riak and Dr. Adhor Arop, opened a clinic. When the doctors
could not handle a problem in the camps, they contacted the UN
for help."

Because of the doctors' commitment and dedication, life
changed for the boys. Dr. Arop, a woman doctor, treated the boys
as if they were her own children. Her counseling and encouragement came from a mother's heart.

"She was a comfort for me. I missed my grandmother and
mother. Dr. Arop gave us love when we hurt so badly from losing
our families," Abraham says. "I missed my grandmother the most
because she had raised me. She was brown color and had beautiful
white teeth. My mother was very black and short, like I am. My
father was lighter skinned than my mother, tall and handsome."

Abraham learned that Sudanese doctors were also assigned to
Itang and Panyadou refugee camps. For some brothers, relief
came too late and many died. The survivors rallied enough

strength to continue another day, but the psychological effects of their ordeal assaulted their tormented minds. Even today, some have never fully recovered; their scars are embedded in a tender part of their hearts where they choose not to visit.

A typical day consisted of cleaning their compounds, then going to school. When school finished, the boys took turns cooking, usually two boys for every ten. Abraham and his brothers grew accustomed to the routine; it felt safe.

Questions poured through Abraham's mind. "Each time I saw a dying friend or I escaped the whims of disease, I realized a higher power held me in a protective embrace. Maybe for a purpose I didn't understand. I wished I knew who cared enough to keep me and the brothers safe."

At the Dimma camp in Ethiopia, Abraham heard about Christianity from the Reverend John Machar Thon. The words of his father explaining the beliefs of their tribal religion had stayed with him through the long journey to Ethiopia. He wondered why he had lived when so many brothers had died.

"I wanted to find out if life promised a reward for those who were good. I took my questions to Reverend Machar, who helped me understand the truth of the Scriptures.

"When I heard John 3:16, that God so loved the world that He gave His only Son Jesus Christ to die for my sins, I believed. Reverend Machar told me if I believed in Jesus Christ, I would live with Him forever in the next life. I desperately needed to know I was loved and that I had a purpose. I was eleven years old when I accepted Jesus Christ as my Lord and Savior."

Machar baptized Abraham. He chose his Christian name— Abraham. "I had no idea who this Abraham was. I just knew he

was a great man of God, and that's what I wanted to be."
Abraham reflects on the happiness of that day. "It was amazing to
think I had become a son of God. I wanted Yai to be there, but
he did not know Jesus. When I thought about my family, I
wished my mother had known Jesus before she died. He is all we
ever need."

After his conversion, Abraham began to study Dinka. He
longed to understand the Bible in his own dialect. Abraham
spoke the language, but he could not read or write it. Learning
the language and singing to God in his own language gave him
peace and comfort. If the church needed any work completed, he
eagerly volunteered.

"I read about the disciples and learned more about God and
His Son. When I read about Paul, how he persecuted the church
and God still called him to preach, I was encouraged to follow
Jesus Christ with all my heart. When I struggled in bitter hate
about what had been done to me and all the difficulties in coming to Ethiopia, question after question filled my mind. Who
saved me in those difficulties? Why didn't I die? Why were so
many other people killed? I realized that God had a plan for me.
I was so happy to know that He came as my Savior."

The other camps also had pastors. At Itang camp, Father
Dominic Matong and the Reverend Peter Bol served God and the
people. At Panyadou, the Reverend Mayol Ajak told the Lost
Boys about Jesus. These men of God, representing different
denominations, preached to all the camps. Many people were
converted to Christianity.

Once Abraham became a Christian, he had hope for his life.
The biggest change came in a love for all people. He began to

share the gospel with his brothers, telling them that God loved them, but He would punish them for not following Him. Abraham looked and felt healthier, and for the first time, he was happy. If he died, he would die in the Lord and be with Him.

"My faith gave me some challenges, but I never became discouraged."

Abraham told the others they all belonged to one community of God. The Lost Boys came from different areas, different languages, different cultures, and the war in Sudan had brought them to Ethiopia, but the only thing that would keep them together was to be one in Christ. Some of the boys were already Christians on the journey to Ethiopia. They understood the power of God, but this new way of thinking and living filled Abraham with hope and a vision for the future.

While in Ethiopia, a few Arabs joined them because they felt the GOS was wrong in its treatment of those who refused to convert to Islam. Abraham opened his heart to them, too, pointing out to others that all men are creations of God.

Gradually the conditions in Ethiopia grew better. Schools were established, first beneath the trees to escape the sweltering sun, then later in the shelter of grass huts, which Abraham and his brothers helped to construct.

"I was happy. Life was good."

The United Nations trained most of the teachers. They were Sudanese and Ethiopians who had attended school and valued the importance of an education. Some of their teachers had come from SPLA.

The schools taught English, Arabic, math, science, geography, and agriculture. Although the teachers had very few books, they taught what they already knew. The boys wrote their lessons in the dirt and used rocks, sticks, and other primitive means of conveying what they learned. They acquired the skills to live independently through the hardships of refugee life.

"My desire for education began in Ethiopia. I realized that only knowledge would help me and my brothers overcome the obstacles and tragedies of our lives."

Abraham was a member of a proud race, and he was determined to not fail God or his people of southern Sudan. He hungered for God's Word, and he hungered for education.

Four years later in 1991, government unrest came to Ethiopia when powers changed. Abraham vividly remembers the rebels—the new government of Ethiopia.

"I heard the gunshots about eight o'clock one morning in the Dimma camp. The fighting grew louder. I didn't want to believe it. Everything that happened in my village suddenly rose in my mind. I was scared, but I would do what I could to live. I grabbed my Bible and fled with my brothers."

Many years later, when Abraham reflects on that tragic day, he believes the rebel soldiers didn't set out to kill the Lost Boys, but instead they looked for those who opposed the new government within the refugee camps. "They [Ethiopian soldiers] captured some of the brothers and took them to the United Nations or to a hospital."

The rebel soldiers used guns and bombs to drive Abraham and the brothers from the Ethiopian border. Again they faced the Gilo River, which separated Ethiopia from Sudan. Where once friendly Ethiopians had brought boats to help them across, the boys were now on their own.

Abraham stood on the banks and stared at the blue, wide river, plagued by strong currents and crocodiles. Fear gripped him as strong as when he had first encountered his destroyed village four years earlier. Behind him the crack of rifle fire and the cries of the wounded pierced his ears. He knew how to swim. Trembling, he prayed for God to protect him and his brothers. Abraham jumped into the river and made it to the other side with his Bible intact. He was one of the first boys to swim to the other side.

"Crocodiles did not come near me," Abraham says. "I didn't see any until I had already crossed. Only by God did I escape death. He kept me safe."

In an effort to help those fleeing the refugee camps, a few Ethiopians strung a rope across the river. It broke from the weight of the boys crossing, hurling them into the river. To stay behind on the bank of the Gilo meant death or imprisonment; to cross the churning river invited drowning and provoked the waiting crocodiles. For the ones who managed to swim across the river and dared to look behind, two thousand floating bodies added to their anguish.

"When I looked back, I saw the Gilo River had turned red with my brothers' blood. My good friend Deng Wol died in the river. I couldn't find Yai. I hurt so much for all, but for Yai and Deng my heart ached. I cried. Many of my brothers I never saw again."

On the opposite bank, the boys were still within firing range. Exhausted, Abraham and some of the brothers ran. Many could not run, so they crawled for miles to flee the bullets from rebel soldiers. Once more they had to survive by their own wits: skirting the elements, the enemy, and wild animals. To the Lost Boys, all sought to destroy and devour them. Would they ever find a haven?

William Deng, a Lost Boy currently living in Texas, recalls that horrible day as clearly as Abraham does: "The booming of artilleries, whizzing of bullets, and the bloody sight I experienced in the wars in the Sudan remained intact in my brain. Days and nights passed by as those horrible images kept replaying in my mind. I am not sure whether I was mad or normal."

Some of the boys elected to return to their own villages and towns in southern Sudan. Other brothers forged on to Pochalla and Pakok, outposts for the SPLA. Abraham went to Pakok. There, he found little food, not enough to keep anyone alive for very long. However, the men, women, and children living there opened their arms to the boys and did whatever they could to help them.

"All the memories of the past when I walked with my brothers to Ethiopia stayed in my mind," Abraham says. "I didn't want to starve or be killed by enemy fire. God had seen me through the dangers before, and I believed He would again. I prayed. I read my Bible. And I prayed some more."

The boys resorted to eating plants, leaves from trees, roots, and whatever else they could find. To Abraham and the brothers, life looked no better than it had four years before. Every day they encountered another hindrance in the struggle to survive.

"It was almost harder this time because we knew the difficulties from before," Abraham says. "I encouraged the others. John 3:16 comforted me more than any other verse from the Bible."

Later Abraham learned the GOS denied the United Nations access to Pochalla and Pakok, stating it would bomb the area and the UN officials if they brought food and supplies to towns known to house SPLA.

Despite the threats, a few months afterward, the International Rescue Committee (IRC) brought aid to the needy children in Pochalla and Pakok. But that, too, came to an end when the SPLA and GOS forces clashed, and the boys fled both towns with enemy forces close behind.

"Enemy soldiers chased us farther into the semidesert region. Much of southern Sudan is green and beautiful, a paradise, but that is not where we were."

The GOS soldiers shot many of the brothers until the soldiers tired of the pursuit. If they trailed the Lost Boys much farther, the GOS would encounter the SPLA. The GOS soldiers chose to allow the desert environment and wild animals to deal with the refugee problem.

Abraham shakes his head. "Always the enemy thought we were a part of the SPLA."

Several scorching days passed under the Sudan sun as Abraham and the brothers once again faced the perils of living in the desert and wild. Without food or water, many decided the inevitable would occur. All they could do was lie in the desert and wait for death.

"Many of the Christian brothers believed God heard our pleas when a miracle happened." Abraham smiles. "A UN water truck found us."

Abraham and his brothers were near death. The driver contacted other drivers and more trucks arrived. The drivers carried the unresponsive boys inside the vehicles and transported them to Lokichokio, Kenya.

"I was so happy to stay in Kenya because I was tired of running, the killing, and facing insecurity all the time. I knew the

IRC and the UNHCR [United Nations High Commission for Refugees] would give us food and medical attention." Abraham again had hope and for the moment he felt safe.

Have my people always been persecuted? Abraham wondered. He longed to learn the history of Sudan in hopes of finding out why civil war had raged for so long in his country.

Do not fear, for I am with you;
do not be afraid, for I am your God.
I will strengthen you; I will help you;
I will hold on to you with My righteous right hand.

ISAIAH 41:10

Chapter Four

A Land Torn by Conflict

Once Abraham grasped the history of Sudan, he better understood the political atmosphere surrounding the critical issues plaguing his country. He saw the problems—problems that could not be solved unless the leaders of both the north and south were committed to lasting peace. The lingering question in Abraham's mind was how could Sudan rise from the years of hatred and strife to work together for the good of the people.

The plight of southern Sudan did not occur in the last few decades but, rather, in a series of events spanning several hundred years. Sudan cradles a vast heritage of Arab and black Africans who share a common country but little else. Different races, different languages, and different cultures breed disharmony beyond the physical boundaries of north and south Sudan. The history is laden with political unrest, religious differences, bloodshed, and selfish interests.

"To understand the situation in my country, I had to study the history and that meant going back to the Bible," Abraham says.

The Bible references to Cush, also known as Ethiopia, are geographically the same as present-day Sudan. This area is mentioned in Genesis, 2 Kings, Esther, Job, Psalms, Isaiah, Jeremiah, Ezekiel, Amos, Nahum, Zephaniah, and Acts. In the book of Numbers, Moses is criticized by his sister Miriam for marrying a Cushite woman. In Acts, the disciple Philip explained Scripture to an Ethiopian eunuch and subsequently baptized him.

"The history shows that the God of the universe established His presence in Sudan," Abraham says. "My homeland became a community of faith hundreds of years before Muhammad was born."

Early Greek recordings indicate the Nubian kings converted to Christianity around AD 540 when Empress Theodora of the Byzantine Empire sent missionaries to preach the gospel. Christianity flourished during this time. Three territories south of the Byzantine province of Egypt along the Nile River rose to distinction. The northern portion lay along southern Egypt and was referred to as Nubia. Beyond this area lay the Makoritae kingdom and farther south the kingdom of Alodaei with its capital near Khartoum, which is Sudan's capital today. Warrior kings ruled these territories, and the people were called Nubians.

In 640, Egypt fell under Arab-Muslim rule, and in 641, Muslims entered Nubia in an attempt to conquer these lands, but the early Christians stopped their advances for hundreds of years. The two groups kept an unsteady peace by exchanging Arab grain for Sudanese slaves. Later the Nubians added ivory, gems, gum arabic, and cattle in exchange for horses and goods from Egypt. Travel and waterways were significant as nomadic Arabs and merchants moved into the Nubian lands. Nubia practiced a matriarchal tradition in the line of succession to the throne, which permitted kings who were not of royal birth. This practice paved the way for Muslims to overpower the throne.

Even in those ancient days, Islamic influence was the major factor in separating northern and southern Sudan. In the more heavily populated areas of the north, followers of Islam encouraged education, expanded trade, and instilled their political values according to the teachings of the Muslim prophet Muhammad.

Political unrest mounted over the control of Egypt, Nubia, and southern black Sudan, creating turmoil for hundreds of years. The spread of Islam and disagreements regarding religious and political views within different sects flamed the upheaval. Arab slave traders raided the south, proving it to be the most lucrative business, while other Arab merchants sought ivory and gum arabic. The southerners despised the northerners who invaded their land and carried away their people and natural resources.

In 1517, the Turks seized control of Egypt and merged the country into the Ottoman Empire. They then controlled the seaports and trading centers of northern Nubia. During this same time, the Funj of the south, a new power controlled by a black sultanate, incorporated dependent tribes and chieftains into one loose band. The Funj assigned areas as tribal lands to the many southern groups. These groups in turn took on tribal identifications. Different tribes today can be traced back to this period. The Funj's power lasted until the early nineteenth century.

From 1821 to 1885, the Turks, needing to expand their own forces, elected to build an army to defend Egypt by using slaves from Sudan. A period of disorder followed as Sudanese Muslims and the Turkish Muslims disagreed in regards to Islamic practices.

The natural boundaries of the Bahr al-Ghazal River and the Sobat River kept the north and south separated. These waterways halted the influx of Islam until the nineteenth century. In 1860, Egypt, under the influence of the British, prohibited slave trading. This angered the Arab traders who had grown wealthy and had no intentions of abandoning the practice.

After 1874, the British urged the Turks, who controlled Egypt, to abolish the slave trade in northern Sudan and to build their military on European methods that excluded slavery. By 1877, the British forcefully ended the practice and added the area of southern Sudan to their empire. Through the years, the British had their share of problems with illegal traders and various Islamic figures who rose to power in an effort to overthrow the British and Turkish rule in Egypt and Sudan. After a series of bloody battles, the Muslims found success in their jihad, or holy war, to gain control of the two countries.

The first Sudanese national government demanded all Sudanese adhere to the Muslim rule or be destroyed. This was known as the mahdist regime after the Muslim leader who called himself the *mahdi* (divinely inspired guide) and who led the Arab Sudanese to victory. He endorsed the Islamic movement and made changes in Sudan in accordance with his visions from Allah. The *mahdi* died of typhoid six months after seizing control, but the government continued to spread Islam through jihad.

During the Muslim reign, the country suffered greatly. Half of the people perished from famine, disease, persecution, and warfare. In the early 1890s, the British launched another campaign to regain control of Sudan in an effort to occupy the Nile. Not until 1899, did the British overcome the Sudanese Arab forces. The British worked to improve peoples' way of life and rebuild the country.

From 1899 to 1955, the Britain and Egypt oversaw the rule of Sudan in a condominium rule. From Khartoum, Britain appointed a governor general to handle Sudanese affairs. Later, British officials formed a council to assist the governor. The council established authority by imposing taxes, ruling over internal affairs, and bringing in modern ideas. Although some of the Sudanese rebelled, the revolts were brought under control. Sudan's eastern, southern, and western boundaries were fixed, settling disputes with neighboring countries.

The British built the economy around the Nile and settled communities in northern Sudan. They built railways and telegraph lines only in these areas, isolating the advancing commercial development of the north and discouraging growth in the south.

Meanwhile, in 1922, Britain approved Egypt's independence, but this did not include Sudan, which remained under Britain's jurisdiction. During the next eighteen years, Sudan remained quiet; however, the Arab elite of Khartoum felt Sudan needed to be independent.

Until after World War I, the British gave little heed to southern Sudan, other than to squelch tribal disputes and discourage slave trade. They defended this policy by stating the south was not ready for modern advances. The north enjoyed the benefits of modernization, both economic and political, while the south remained hundreds of years behind.

The British colonial administration closed southern Sudan to much of everything except Christian missionaries and schools. Roman Catholics, Presbyterians, and the Anglican Church Missionary Society were the largest groups. The government did finally subsidize schools for the south, but the north considered those educated in the south inferior.

After 1920, the British discouraged the Muslim religion, Arab dress, and Arab customs and forbade northern Sudanese to work in the south. The British encouraged black tribal traditions—all with the idea of a separate north and south. In 1930, the British proclaimed that the blacks of southern Sudan were to be considered a separate people from the northern Muslims. Many believed this was to prepare the south for an eventual incorporation into British East Africa.

Government officials in the north vehemently protested when the British stipulated the south's resources were to remain in that part of the country. Southern Sudan was rich agriculturally, and the isolation of the area hindered economic growth for the north. Ruling parties in the north followed Muslim Arab ideals, and the governing bodies in the south took on the mindset of the British East African colonies.

After World War I, Sudanese nationalism grew with the Arab Muslims of the north, pushing the British for a unified Sudan and a Muslim government. Strangely enough, the first prime minister of Sudan was a Muslim Dinka, Ali Abd al Latif, who worked for a unified Sudan that would share governing powers with a combination of religious leaders in the north and tribal leaders in the south, but his idea did not gain popularity.

In the 1930s, neither Britain nor Egypt would agree to an independent Sudan. Over the next few decades, conflict continued regarding the north's dominance over the south's cultural, traditional, and political interests.

In 1948, the British allowed a representative of both regions to form a legislative assembly. Again, Egypt protested an independent Sudan, claiming it as a part of Egypt. In 1953, Britain and Egypt agreed that both would withdraw their military forces from Sudan over a three-year period and give the country the right to self-government. Despite continuing conflict between north and south, Sudan gained its independence in 1956.

Political clashes in the north concerned Egyptian involvement in Sudan. In 1958, a military coup toppled the government. The new ruling power nullified all political parties.

Southern Sudan protested Arab influence in the south but felt the issues could be handled through negotiations in Khartoum rather than through violence. The United States pledged its support for the new country and offered aid to improve economic and technological conditions by expanding transportation and communication. When the economy did not meet the country's expectations, more unrest followed.

During 1964–69, opposition to the northern government escalated. The regime in Khartoum dissolved and was replaced by a civil servant who opened the way to political parties. Many of these parties rose through various political interests throughout the country, creating more disorder. With the increased fighting, it is estimated that in 1964, sixty thousand Sudanese refugees fled to Uganda, with seven thousand leaving in a ten-day period. Southern guerrilla movements extended the turmoil to rural areas, forcing the government to seek ways to end the conflict.

In 1965, the new civilian government launched a military campaign to end the rebellion in the south where many civilians had been brutally murdered. The government soldiers burned homes, churches, and schools and destroyed cattle and crops.

In 1969, another military coup, led by Col. Jaafar al-Nimeiri, took control of the government. In the same year, various foreign powers supplied weapons, aid, supplies, and training to the southern guerrilla forces. The rebels hit at random. They confiscated weapons, food, and supplies from the northern government. Time and again, efforts for peace talks failed with Khartoum responding by sending additional troops in an attempt to overcome the southern forces.

Sudan adopted an official flag on May 20, 1970. It consisted of three horizontal bands in red, white, and black with a green isosceles triangle on the hoist side. These were the pan-Arab colors adopted by Syria in March 1920. Red signified struggles and Islamic martyrs in the Sudan and Arab lands. White represented peace, optimism, light, and love. Black represented the Sudan and the *mahdija* revolution of the nineteenth century, and green stood for Islamic prosperity and agriculture.

In 1971, Joseph Lagu, took control of the southern guerrilla movement by creating the Southern Sudanese Liberation Movement (SSLM). In 1972, Sudan's first civil war ended with the Addis Ababa agreement. This document was hailed as the perfect peace plan for a united country separated by so many issues. The agreement gave the north ultimate jurisdiction over international and national policy and allowed the south control of its oil and its own government. The problems still existed, but the north and south were committed to working out their differences.

Al-Nimeiri appointed a committee to form a permanent constitution, despite opposition from political and religious leaders in Khartoum. This constitution named Islam as Sudan's main religion but also made stipulations for Christianity to be practiced freely. Al-Nimeiri assumed greater military control to oppose those who demonstrated against his leadership. After his reelection to a second term in 1977, he worked more for a unified Sudan by appealing to southern needs and concerns. When his government was accused of corrupt practices, he established a dictatorship to reinforce his political authority and advocate the *shari'a,* the code of law adhering to Islamic laws and practices.

In 1983, al-Nimeiri realized the tremendous surge of power in the south and moved to tighten Khartoum's hold. The Sudan People's Liberation Movement (SPLM) and the SPLA of the south revolted against President al-Nimeiri's decision to break the Addis Ababa agreement. At the end of 1983, the situation in the south had deteriorated to civil war status again.

During these events in Sudan, Abraham and other Lost Boys were born in this country of turmoil—in the southern land besieged by persecution and bloodshed.

On April 6, 1985, a new military government in Khartoum overthrew al-Nimeiri and abolished the old constitution. Although the new president, Abd ar Rahman Siwar adh Dhahab, promised to end the civil war and establish peace and civilian control in the next year, he was unable to follow through. Sudan's economy sank to poor conditions, and famine spread throughout

the south and west. Dhahab could not secure needed funds to
bail out his country, and most of the funds received were used to
combat the southern rebellion. The famine claimed between four
hundred thousand and five hundred thousand lives while the civil
war escalated. Dhahab attempted to reconcile with the south, but
his demands did not meet with the approval of the SPLA leader,
John Garang. Still peace negotiations forged ahead in the midst
of the fighting.

Political, economic, and religious differences stood in the way
of a unified Sudan. On June 30, 1989, Umar Hassan Ahmad al-
Bashir took control of the country. He issued a commitment to
end the civil war militarily by imposing the *shari'a* for the non-
Muslim south. Peace efforts would be thwarted for a long time as
the northern forces persisted in dropping bombs on southern
civilians.

On April 26, 2002, former Senator John C. Danforth, a U.S.
special envoy for peace, issued his report ("The Outlook for Peace
in Sudan") to President George W. Bush. Danforth twice visited
Sudan and met with Sudanese officials and the SPLA. He saw
firsthand the starving and persecuted civilians. He conducted
interviews and listed the civil war and human rights as the most
important concerns. Peace could be achieved only by the north
and south abandoning warfare and establishing areas for humanitarian organizations to offer aid. Danforth recommended international involvement and monitoring in the peace process. He
believed past agreements were nothing more than pieces of paper,
none of which had initiated actions involving permanent peace.
Both north and south indicated they wanted a peaceful end to the
conflict and invited American involvement.

The GOS and the SPLM/SPLA met in Machakos, Kenya, in June 2002 with a pledge to peace talks. Both sides committed to negotiate a peaceful resolution for a unified Sudan, although reports indicate that fighting between the north and south continued to occur. During the Machakos peace talks, critics cited human rights violations against the southern Sudanese. Peace negotiators attempted to guide the Khartoum government and the SPLA/SPLM to allow humanitarian aid into war-torn areas.

"The southern Sudanese pray for the problems to be resolved," Abraham says. "Many of the Lost Boys who have family and friends living in Sudan long for the pastoral life they knew as young boys. Fear, disease, and starvation have accompanied them more than the memories of a loving family."

As much as Abraham would like to see a democratic government for his people, democracy is a difficult concept for those who live there. Government leadership is associated with whomever has the ability to gain and maintain control. In the event the Sudanese were permitted to elect their leaders, the qualified people are mainly the elite, educated Arab Muslims in the north, who have the knowledge necessary to keep the country from economic ruin. The same type of regime would continue—with the approval of the population. The theory of self-government has little chance of success until all the people are educated. The Lost Boys are gaining education in various fields that will allow them to lead and serve their country. Abraham questions how the people would be governed fairly in the interim process. How would a government undertake mass education?

Abraham remembers President Bush signing the Sudan Peace Act into law on October 21, 2002. This document denounces the

Sudanese government's use of slavery and genocide as weapons of war. It states that in the event the government does not actively participate in good-faith peace talks with the southern rebel movement, the United States administration will cease political relations with Khartoum, actively discourage monetary aid and assistance from international sources, oppose Sudan's oil profitability, and approach the United Nations for an arms embargo.

"I have today signed into law H.R. 5531, the Sudan Peace Act," the president said. "This act demonstrates the clear resolve of the United States to promote a lasting, just peace; human rights; and freedom from persecution for the people of Sudan. The Act is designed to help address the evils inflicted on the people of Sudan by their government—including senseless suffering, use of emergency food relief as a weapon of war, and the practice of slavery—and to press the parties, and in particular the Sudanese government, to complete in good faith the negotiations to end the war."[1]

Abraham realizes that conducting unbiased negotiations with a primary focus on human rights and dignity is a difficult task for any mediator involved with the Sudan situation. The United States and European allies who are committed to this operation must address every issue involving humanitarian aid.

In December 2002, the Sudan's Organization against Torture (SOAT) reported that although both sides were adhering to the cease-fire, religious persecution, including torture and random arrests, was still occurring among those who opposed the government.

A new agreement was signed in February 2003, while talks proceeded in Machakos. Meanwhile, humanitarian organizations trying to aid displaced people have been denied access to war-torn areas. In addition, the Civilian Protection Monitoring Team (CPMT) had not been able to enter the areas necessary for investigation and reports. Both skeptics and optimists keep their attention focused on the peace talks in the twenty-year-old civil war.

Amnesty International and Human Rights Watch, as well as other humanitarian organizations, appealed to the UN Commission on Human Rights for continued monitoring in Sudan.

In April 2003, the UN's human rights commission in Geneva, Switzerland, upgraded Khartoum's status and declared the situation in Sudan no longer needed consideration. In the midst of Machakos peace talks, world terrorism reports focused on Khartoum's relationship to al-Qaeda and Osama bin Laden.

At times the peace negotiations appeared to collapse, despite the sincere efforts of chief mediator Lazaro Sumbeiywo of the Inter Governmental Authority on Development (IGAD). In July 2003, Khartoum rejected Sumbeiywo's peace draft and criticized the Machakos negotiators, but the talks resumed on July 23 in Nakuru, Kenya. As the summer months plodded ahead, war again looked imminent. As August moved into September, oil revenue sharing was a heated topic in the peace talks as well as security issues in protecting the south from Khartoum's military dominance.

A breakthrough occurred on September 25, 2003, when senior representatives from Khartoum and the SPLA/SPLM agreed on "security arrangements." However, peace talks have not established an agreement. As of this writing, bombing and fighting still occur, especially in the oil rich areas. Skeptics fear the delay in the peace process decreases the likelihood of Khartoum and the SPLA establishing peace.

Wal and Julia Duany founded South Sudanese Friends International (SSFI) in 1994 to work for peace and assistance for the people in south Sudan. Julia Duany has seen their suffering from warfare. She says, "Is it any wonder that the grassroots people of southern Sudan—the common people of the villages—have given up on empty political promises of a better future? More than a decade of war has taught them that money spent on machine guns and land mines does not return the same dividend that comes from money invested in food production, health care, and education. The common people have lost everything to the war, but they have learned something important: Their future lies within themselves."[2]

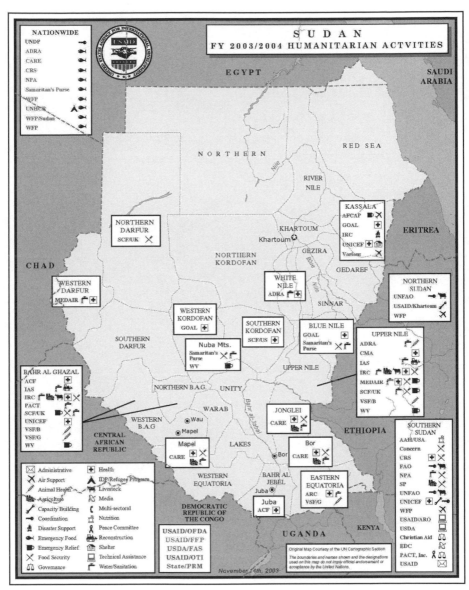

Map courtesy of USAID, www.usaid.gov; used with permission.

The world has been deceived that the war in Sudan is nothing more than tribal disputes. Two million people have died in Sudan not because of tribal wars but because of the government's intent to eliminate the black Africans.

ABRAHAM NHIAL

Chapter Five
Sudan People's Liberation Army

James Okuk Solomon, a Lost Boy of the Shilluk tribe, was born in 1974 to an educated father and an uneducated mother in a large village called Palo. The village lies in Dollieb Hill district of Upper Nile State, as it is now known.

"By the time I was born, many of the inhabitants of Palo village had embraced Christianity from the Presbyterian Church's evangelization. The French company, which had started to dig the Jongli canal, gave the Palo people many job opportunities and taught them new technology in different fields. From this technology, the village progressed so fast that it became known as the civilized village of the Shilluk kingdom. Even the Nuer tribe called it the Khartoum of Shilluk. From thatched huts, people began to build zinc squares. More schools were built besides those of the church, and almost every child enjoyed the free primary education while practicing the other common village activities.

"It is during this time of relative peace, after the Addis Ababa agreement had been signed, that I was born and began to grow up as a child of a village but with a civilized mentality. I enjoyed life with my parents, brothers, sisters, cousins, aunts, uncles, grandparents, and the dwellers of the village. I looked after goats and cattle, went fishing and hunting, gathered gums and edible fruits in the forest, and cultivated during the rainy season and gardened along the river. I attended public village ceremonies and dances at an early age. Besides these [activities] I went to church and followed my parents' spirituality.

"Everything was loving and enjoyable, and I felt safe in every home of the village. There was no sense of hunger, thirst, disease, or war except the fear of wild animals. Death took the lives of old people and rarely younger people. Indeed, the village looked like heaven or the Garden of Eden as described in the Bible. Everybody was happy. Foreigners were hosted without any suspicion, and you could tell that it was the best possible village that God could ever create."

James's story takes a sad note. In 1984, the worst possible horror occurred in the village when Muslim-led government soldiers attacked and burned the village. James hid and watched it all.

He remembers those who were captured by the soldiers received a fate worse than those who were caught in the burning village. Their limbs and body parts were severed until the pain killed them. "Even the external parts of reproductive organs were cut and forced into mouths and noses. Some people were stripped naked and forced to have sex regardless of the gender." The evil soldiers mocked those suffering. When the soldiers completed their inhumane treatment, they killed the remaining villagers, then pushed the bodies into the river. Others were beheaded. The heads were thrown into the fire, and the soldiers made fun of the bursting sound of their brains. The soldiers did the same to small babies.

When the soldiers believed everyone was dead, they left the village singing praises to Allah and the holy war. James says the songs meant the soldiers had cleansed the area of infidels so they (the soldiers) could go to paradise.

As evening approached, hyenas fed on the dead bodies. James found the strength to stand and run from the hyenas, but he had no idea where he was headed. The atrocities done to his people went far beyond what a child should ever see or learn about. The sound of his own feet caused him to run the entire night; he thought the hyenas chased him. After daybreak, he began to feel the pain of the thorns that had pricked his blood-covered feet. He began to pull them out, but some were too hard for his fingers. He cried until no more tears flowed.

"I thought of the hyenas coming after me, and the soldiers looking to murder me after the genocide. This gave me survival courage and energy to move ahead where I could find a refuge. It was very hard to put my hurting feet on the ground, but there was no other option of possible survival so I had to go on limping until late evening. I didn't know where I was except that I was in a forest. I could not tell which direction I was moving."

James continued limping through the darkness of the second night and found a village inhabited by Dinkas. Soon a woman appeared carrying a gun. He could not understand the woman, and she could not understand him. She brought him inside her home, gave him water, and prepared food for him, but James refused to eat. The thoughts of what he'd witnessed in his village sickened him.

As he became more aware of his surroundings, James noticed the village was void of men. He wondered what had happened to them. "Later I learned the SPLA took all the men away to be recruited as fighters. They left the old men who did not have the energy to fight."

Days passed, and the SPLA soldiers returned to the village looking for additional people to help them in the war. Most of the original men and boys had been killed in battle. The soldiers decided to recruit the women and children. James went with them. The small band walked for nearly a month to the training camp in Itang, Ethiopia. Along the way, enemy soldiers attacked them, killing ten of the small group. Half were children, and James received a minor leg wound. No one took the time to bury the dead.

At the camp in Itang, the children were separated from the women so they could be trained as child soldiers. "The soldiers named the children the 'Red Army' because they were trained to be merciless to the enemy and whoever opposed the SPLA leadership. Some of them were to be the bodyguards and watchdogs of the commanders."

The child soldiers graduated after three months of training. Their guns took priority over everything. James said the guns became their parents and friends. The children believed the weapons would take care of all their needs. "We were also told to be trigger-happy because that would be the only way we could achieve our wants. I was so small that the gun was equal height to me, but I was happy to have it because I planned to take revenge on those who had hurt me and driven me away."

Often James stole away from the training camp to join different fighting battalions. He fought fiercely and courageously. All he cared about was revenge. The commander asked James to be his bodyguard, but he refused to obey the man's orders. James thought being a bodyguard would not give him the opportunity to repay the evil done to him. The soldiers nicknamed James "Small Hitler." Young and old admired his military courage.

In one attack on Juba Town, James was wounded and taken to Lokichokio, Kenya, for treatment. This became a positive turn in his life. Human rights activists detained him in Lokichokio. They stated James was still a child and too young to be a soldier.

The activists placed James in school. He despised it and viewed education as a waste of time. He thought that only a gun had the power to make an educated man kneel down before him. He shouldn't be denied a gun or the chance to fight the enemy. At the school, nearly everyone seemed to hate him because he'd rather fight than talk. During those first few weeks, he hoped the school would dismiss him, but that didn't happen.

Despite a poor start, James did finish his education and later received a master's degree in sociopolitical ethics from Catholic University of Eastern Africa in Nairobi, Kenya, in 2004.

Abraham values the work of the dedicated members of the SPLA. They are committed soldiers who fight with no pay in an effort to end the suffering, persecution, and violence in southern Sudan.

"The prognosis in Sudan is by no means reassuring. Crisis succeeds crisis, yet the leaders come up with few solutions. In my opinion, a man's ability to make and maintain enduring friendships will be in the measure of his ability to lead. A leader is the one with the ability to meet the unpleasant, the enemy, or even devastating facts and situations without panic. He must also be willing to take firm action when necessary, even if it is unpopular." Abraham believes that a Christian leader must have a testimony and be sensitive to the needs of people and compassionate in dealing with them.

Lt. Col. John Garang formed the SPLA in 1983 when the northern government in Khartoum sent him to Bor in southern Sudan with orders to stop an insurrection. Five hundred southern soldiers refused placement in the north. Instead of using force, Garang rallied the soldiers and urged them to resist not only in Bor but also in other areas of the south. He defied his orders from the GOS and set himself up as commander of the southern rebel movement.

Those who have studied Garang state he is a highly respected and formidable leader, capable and driving. He is an educated man and values the needs of the southern Sudanese. Although Garang is the prime leader of the largest southern guerrilla army in the south, other warlords operate separate from the SPLA's command. What these independent warlords accomplish, whether for the good or detriment of southern interests, is usually attributed to the SPLA/SPLM.

Prior to his activities with the SPLA, Garang was born into a Christian Dinka family and studied at Grinnell College in Iowa. Later he took a company commanders' course at Fort Benning, Georgia, and received an advanced economics degree at Iowa State University.

Initially, the SPLA aspired to a united Sudan with the south maintaining religious freedom and some self-government. Since then, reports indicate it is advocating for more autonomy and possibly independence from the north.

Forty battalions within the SPLA's guerrilla forces comprise approximately sixty thousand soldiers. Some reports indicate a much smaller figure. These battalions are named after animals, birds, and reptiles. Promotion within the army is based on seniority and the number of battles, and all the leaders are members of the southern tribes of Sudan.

Critics say the SPLA has killed innocent civilians. According to those who oppose the guerrilla army, these actions prove, once again, innocent people suffer the cruelest effects of war. SPLA opponents claim the SPLA abducts boys and young men to fill its army. Children from all over Sudan are found in military service for the GOS and SPLA, although the United Nations condemns the practice of child soldiers.

"Those boys who seek to fight with the SPLA do so out of revenge for their murdered families and friends," Abraham says. "They want to be a part of the guerrilla army, although the United Nations forbids it. Many will do anything to be a part of the soldiers."

The war effort takes priority over many crucial needs of the entire country: medical attention, food, proper housing, and sanitary conditions. Reports from some humanitarian organizations state many of the prisoners captured during combat by the GOS and the SPLA are killed as well as civilians who are believed to be informers. The reports conflict because much of the information stems from the civil strife.

Abraham says southern Sudan has a legitimate fear and distrust of the GOS. While the Lost Boys lived in the Ethiopian refugee camps, some Arabs joined the SPLA because they felt the south was justified in its rebellion. The SPLA isn't out to eliminate the GOS soldiers; its mission is to free all of Sudan from Muslim oppression. The country is diverse, and the SPLA understands the importance of peace and cooperation among a culturally diverse people.

"The mission of the SPLA is for every person to have freedom of speech, beliefs, worship, and freedom. If one of the tribes in Sudan wants to rule the country and impose their particular culture, for instance, Muslim culture, it is wrong," Abraham says.

Critics also state that the SPLA loots villages in the south for food and supplies.

"It is important for people to know that the guerrilla army does not have an organized handbook of rules and guidelines; neither are they paid. When the soldiers are hungry and a village doesn't share what they have, the provisions are taken," Abraham says. "The villagers fail to see that if the SPLA are hungry, they cannot protect and fight for southern Sudan. What else can they do? The soldiers can't stop to plant crops. It's an unfortunate situation for a country that is on the brink of starvation. The SPLA, the people of southern Sudan, all need food. Other needs are crucial, such as medical care and military supplies. The list is endless."

In essence, the SPLA is advocating religious freedom for all of Sudan and a sharing of the economy and resources. Many supporters of the SPLA and the war believe the best way to achieve this status is through a separate southern Sudan.

Abraham says the GOS has a term for the black African— *abid,* which means black slave. GOS policy is to kill the *abid* with the *abid.* In other words, a village of black Africans is forced into the Muslim religion. That village, in turn, wars on another tribe to force its people into the Muslim faith. Infiltration breeds more infiltration. World leaders need to see what is really happening. The conflicts are not tribal disputes but are caused by directives issued by the government.

Supporters of the guerrilla army praise the SPLA's dedication to free the south from Khartoum's tyranny. The soldiers are acclaimed as heroes and welcomed into homes and villages.

The Lost Boys have varied opinions about the SPLA according to their experiences with the guerrilla fighting force. Most agree the SPLA is southern Sudan's hope for peace regardless of what critics report about its activities.

The following is testimony about the SPLA from a Lost Boy living in Canada. "I am a member of SPLA, and I will be for as long as it takes; even though I am not in the front line, I am still supporting it. I believe in justice, I believe in freedom, and I believe in peace. We have never experienced justice, freedom, or peace. The people of the south were living in hell prior to SPLA taking up arms. It was worth the effort of that organization to fight the Khartoum regime, for because of it, we have survived despite the fact that millions have died. I believe in its ideals; it is fighting for the right cause. Without the SPLA's presence in the region, we would have been eliminated by the Islamic government.

"The SPLA originated as a response to the cruel rule imposed by the north on us [southern Sudan] for more than forty years, and it is fighting for all maltreated and marginalized people across Sudan. The SPLA wants all people to be treated the same, equally without exception. It is fighting to make people equal despite culture, origin, race, gender, religious beliefs, tribe, or language spoken.

Sudan is a country where more than six hundred ethnic and tribal groups dwell, and with the policy of assimilation and conversion, that nation will never be unified fairly."

In earlier years, the SPLA received weapons from surrounding countries and operated largely within the borders of Ethiopia. Because many cities and towns in southern Sudan are now occupied by the SPLA, the guerrilla forces no longer need to rely on invasion methods from outside their borders. They are not heavily armed and obtain most of their weapons and heavy artillery by capturing government inventory and through negotiations with other allies.

An isolated, strong force of SPLA fighters are located in the Nuba Mountains, an area in south-central Sudan. These soldiers depend on light aircraft for supplies in order to continue the war. In January 2002, the U.S. government mediated a cease-fire for the Nubia front, but reports indicate that fighting still persists. Currently, one of the issues in the peace talks is the control of the Nuba Mountains.

The SPLA focuses its military attacks on government forces in strategic locations, including those areas critical to the oil industry. It has been successful in opening up a large stretch of land from the western border of the Central African Republic to the eastern border of Ethiopia and on northeast to the Eritrean border. Even with these holdings, the guerrilla forces are outnumbered by the GOS.

Abraham believes the Lost Boys are ambassadors for the SPLA. He feels all of the Lost Boys are members. "We need to represent the SPLA in the Western world, by speaking the true mission of the guerrilla army."

"I am convinced that God has sent the Lost Boys out from Sudan and into the world for a purpose—to witness about the horrible conditions in Sudan. We believe in love, living together, and maintaining a Christian identity. We were believers before we came to the United States. The Sudanese churches in the United States have seen that we are on a mission of peace. We thank the American government for the opportunity to come here. We want all Americans to know about the war in Sudan, and our presence is for a purpose—because we are bringing the message of suffering Sudanese to Americans.

"We are here physically, but our minds and spirits are at home with the SPLA. We pray for God to give the SPLA power so we may be free. We pray that all the leaders of the SPLA should open their hearts to God. We are proud of them. They are brave men.

"Many times when the SPLA captures enemy soldiers, they give the prisoners an opportunity to remain in the south where they can be free and worship as they choose. When the Arabs capture our people, they don't take many prisoners of war—they usually kill them. The mission of the south is not to prevent the enemy from their beliefs, but establish a country where there is freedom of worship. We need our land as ours not as slaves. I think it will be almost impossible to share all of Sudan with a people who do not know the truth of where they are going after they die. God says killing is sin, but the Sudanese will continue to war as long as there are Muslims and Christians. We need a new Sudan, governed by God."

Later chapters will examine other factors in the warfare: the Muslim religion, oil, and slavery.

The pastors told us to take one
day at a time and rely only on God.

ABRAHAM NHIAL

Chapter Six

Life in Kakuma

A month after arriving back in Kenya, Abraham and his brothers—a total of sixteen thousand Lost Boys—were transported to Kakuma, a desolate place in northern Kenya named for the short plant that thrives there. The United Nations purchased this land from the Kenyan government to establish a refugee camp for the boys. The desertlike area housed few animals and plant life and did not lend itself to a thriving community for humans. The wind blew the gritting dirt constantly, making it difficult to see, and nothing could be grown there.

"Although I was happy to be in a safe place, some things about Kakuma made life difficult," Abraham says. "We could not cook in the daytime due to the high winds blowing dirt into the food."

Through the assistance of the UNHCR, the boys helped build their new homes and community buildings. They were totally dependent on food and supplies from the United Nations, churches, and humanitarian organizations.

"I wanted to be involved in the building of the camp, so I built my own hut," Abraham recalls. "I didn't want to depend on others if I could find a way to do it. This was not easy. I had little energy from everything that had happened. I dug sixteen holes, then placed short poles inside them to form a square hut. Long poles were nailed together for a roof. Sometimes we hurt ourselves badly. The walls were made of mud, and the dirt mixed with the water contained thorns. This often hurt our feet and hands, and I didn't like this part at all. The huts were small, fitting two maybe three people."

To Abraham, one of the worst parts of camp life was idle time. It made him think too much about the past. Without anything to do, some of the Lost Boys fought with each other or sank into severe depression.

"The pastors and many of the teachers who had lived in the Ethiopian refugee camps had been forced to leave Ethiopia with us and cross the Gilo River. They were with us in Pochalla and Pakok and also driven into the desert."

The pastors provided strength and courage to Abraham and the brothers. "They said God would take care of us. I encouraged my friends to come to church, and they did. There we had Bible study and sang songs. We also learned about church work."

The United Nations provided books for the teachers so the boys could continue their schooling. Abraham and the brothers recalled that education was the means to secure their hopes and dreams.

Kakuma later housed other refugees, primarily from Ethiopia, Somalia, Uganda, Burundi, and the Congo. The camp grew to mammoth proportions. With expansion came conflicts arising from different cultures, religions, languages, and the overwhelming needs of so many people separated from their homes and forced to live in cramped quarters. Violence frequently erupted. Lack of proper sanitation and shortages of medicine ushered in disease. Surrounding villages would raid the refugee camp for supplies. For the Lost Boys, their life spun with turmoil. Kakuma existed as a safer place than Sudan and Ethiopia, but they still lived in fear and instability. They had no other place to go, and no guarantee any other location would be better.

Abraham's source of comfort came from God Almighty. Without a doubt, he and many other Lost Boys would have died if not for divine protection. Abraham rose as their spiritual leader, a prophet to his brothers and a symbol of hope. The Episcopalian Church ordained him a minister, although he had not received formal seminary training.

"From 1992 to 1994, I worked with an Episcopalian church in Zone One of the refugee camp. From 1994 to 2001, I worked as an evangelist in charge of an Episcopalian church in Zone Two. God is good all the time. He is living in us," Abraham told those around him.

"In 1998, while in Kakuma, I met Richard Parkins, who is the director of Episcopal Migration Ministry. He helped and encouraged me to get a high school education. He is one of my best friends."

In 1998, the U.S. Immigration and Naturalization Service (INS) found out about the Lost Boys through Christian missionaries and agreed to qualify four thousand Lost Boys for resettlement in the United States. This was an opportunity for the boys to be delivered from the overcrowded refugee camp to the States where they could secure an education and improve their lifestyle.

INS refugee qualifications are based on an individual's persecution in the past or potentially in the future because of race, religion, nationality, political affiliation, gender, or fear of cultural practices.

To qualify for the program under INS guidelines, the boys could not be older than twenty-one years of age. All the applicants required a medical exam. Abraham and his brothers also faced an interview process. Questions were posed that only a Lost Boy could answer, to eliminate other people who simply wanted to come to the United States. The following questions are a sample from the interviews.

- What happened to you on your walk to Ethiopia?
- When did you arrive there?
- What camp did you live in Ethiopia?
- What happened there?
- Were you in school?
- What did the United Nations do for you in Ethiopia?
- In 1991, what happened?
- What happened at the Gilo River?
- Where did you go after you crossed the Gilo?
- When did you come to Kakuma?

Life in the Kakuma refugee camp was depressing, with an outlook for the future equally as bleak. For many, hope was but a fragile thread. Abraham and the other boys went about their schooling and everyday activities. They longed for an opportunity to travel to the United States, but so many things had gone wrong in the past. They were afraid to believe life could be better.

In 1999, Abraham received a special blessing. Amidst the hardships of refugee life, he met a young woman named Daruka.

"The first time I met her, I thought there was no other girl like her in the world. She was beautiful, responsible, and I loved her ways. She had a personal relationship with Jesus Christ as her Savior, and she worked hard in the church. She was just what I was looking for."

Daruka lived in Zone One, but she and her brothers attended Abraham's church in Zone Two. Her parents, two sisters, and two brothers escaped from Sudan when northern soldiers destroyed their village in 1992. Through church work, Abraham got to know Daruka better, but he said nothing about his growing feelings.

In the same year, Abraham had the opportunity to leave the refugee camp in Kakuma and return home to the Bahr al-Ghazal province for three weeks. He hadn't been there since he fled Sudan and was anxious to see if any of his family members had survived. He flew with Christian missionaries from South Africa who felt a calling to southern Sudan and the area Abraham called home.

"When the UN plane landed, I looked out at the people and cried. Many of them I recognized from before I fled Sudan. They all looked tired, hungry, and sick. I couldn't believe that was how the war had affected my people. I could not leave the plane for several minutes as I wept and prayed for them. How can I help them? I asked God. Finally, I forced myself to leave the plane. The people I remembered did not know me, but I called them by name. When I told them my name, they thought I'd been killed. We cried together."

Abraham learned his cousin Yai had returned to Geer village after the brothers were chased from the refugee camps in Ethiopia. During the intervening time, Abraham believed Yai had not survived. For a moment, Abraham thought he was in a dream. In turn, Yai could not believe his cousin stood before him. He believed Abraham had died like so many of the Lost Boys. The two stared at each other, embraced, and cried.

"We cried because we missed each other since, and we cried because we were full of joy and happiness."

They talked all day and night without taking time to sleep. Time meant nothing now that they knew death had not separated them.

"How is your life?" Abraham asked Yai. "I want to know everything."

"Good. I have a wife and children. And yours?"

"I'm serving God and the brothers in Kakuma, Kenya, at a refugee camp," Abraham said. "I work with the Episcopalian Church."

Yai smiled. "I'm a Christian too. I accepted Jesus as my Savior after I came back to Sudan."

Abraham spent three days in the village with his cousin and his family. He visited Yai's parents and brothers. Everyone was happy to see him because the village was where Abraham's mother was born and where he lived with his grandmother. He remembered happy times there, when Sudan did not know war.

"I also learned my grandmother who had raised me died three years before. I was very sad, for I loved her very much. Her wish was to see me before she died. The people told me my father was still alive, and I wanted to see him very much. I didn't know how to get home because the area was totally unfamiliar. The grass and brush had grown into a forest because the livestock had been killed or stolen. Yai took me to my father's village. First, I went to where my grandmother used to live and was buried, then I went to see my father. It was very emotional because he believed I was dead. We wept together for a long time. My father looked much older but still handsome in appearance. I learned my mother, two sisters, and a brother had been killed in the civil war.

"I took my fourteen-year-old sister back with me to Kakuma for medical treatment. She had suffered with tuberculosis for three years and had not received any medical attention. She now takes medicine and is doing well. Her name is Rebecca Atong Nhial, and she is short with brown skin. Rebecca attends school in Kakuma where she has a better future. Both of us look like our mother. I tried to persuade my father to return with us, but he did not want to leave his home. He believes it is better to die in our homeland than to live somewhere else."

In 2000, while Abraham busied himself with church work and helping his brothers and the other refugees, he asked Daruka to be his girlfriend.

Then the letters from the INS began to arrive. Lists of those who qualified for resettlement in the United States were posted in the center of the refugee camp for all to view. Ninety boys per week would be transported to the United States. To those who met the qualifications, a new life awaited—one that promised many opportunities. Education held the highest priority. The Lost Boys began their arrival in the United States in November 2000. To those left behind, gloom settled like the dust storms that plagued the refugee camp. Those boys were pleased that their brothers had been chosen but saddened for themselves.

"In January 2001, I learned that I had been accepted into the U.S. refugee program," Abraham says. "I was so very happy and excited for the opportunity to come to America. I also thanked

God for His help to pass the process and the tough interview with the INS." He pauses in his story. "However, Daruka wasn't so happy. She thought I might go to the United States and forget about her."

The two spent a little time together before Abraham left for the United States. They talked of marriage, but the future looked uncertain.

God had plans for Abraham, but the burning questions about his country and the suffering people refused to let him alone. Abraham understood the threefold causes of the civil war: religion, politics, and oil. He realized the closely interwoven problems needed educated people to work together for the good of Sudan. Abraham stepped forward to take his place as a part of the solution.

Our Home: The Sudan
This is our Home,
Let peace dwell here,
Let the land be full of
Contentment,
Let love abide here.

Love of one another,
Love of humanity,
Love of life itself,
And love of God.

Let us remember
That as many hands build a
House,
So many minds make a
Nation.
This is our Home, The Sudan.

JULIA AKER DUANY

Don't be deceived, my dearly loved brothers. Every generous act and every perfect gift is from above, coming down from the Father of lights; with Him there is no variation or shadow cast by turning.

JAMES 1:16–17

Chapter Seven

Islam Versus Christianity

Islam, the official religion of Sudan, maintains there is only one God, and he is called Allah. Allah requires complete submission, and Islam views Muhammad as Allah's last and greatest prophet. Followers of this doctrine are called Muslims, which means "one who submits," to the will of Allah. The basis of this religion is found primarily in the Qur'an, a book of alleged revelations given through Muhammad. The faith and practice of Islam encompasses every facet of the Muslim's life. This governs personal, social, and political matters not only specifically religious matters. In fact, these are inseparable.

Abraham and his brothers experienced in graphic reality the horrific effects of refusing to submit to the Islamic religion. Their homes were destroyed, their families murdered, their sisters sold into slavery, and their lives altered forever in the midst of the current civil war. Many Sudanese who fall under Khartoum's military regime are given the choice of surrendering to Muslim beliefs or for-feiting their lives. Others are denied food, water, and medical atten-tion unless they yield to the mandates of the Muslim government. The Sudanese who survive the bombings and raids are escorted to displacement camps. These government facilities are located in iso-lated areas with little food, water, shelter, or medical attention.

Abraham's opinion is that when Muslims are a minority they are a good, respectable people. When Muslims become a major-ity, they are dangerous. "Christians must pay attention to how the Muslims work at converting others to Islam."

As stated in chapter 4, history depicts the ongoing conflict between the Islamic regime and those who oppose the Muslim way of life. This chapter presents some of the basic differences between Islam and Christianity in order to create a better under-standing of why these atrocities are happening in Sudan and throughout the world today.

Islamic Doctrine

The term *Allah* means "the divinity" in Arabic. For the Arab Muslim, Allah is the one and only God. For the Muslim or the Christian, God is the God of Abraham, Moses, and Jesus; how-ever, the Muslim adds Muhammad to its list of authentic teach-ers. Muhammad is the true authority for the Muslim, although he was a human who admitted to committing sins.

Muslims believe in one God, creator of all things, the prophets of the Bible, Jesus and His second coming, the Bible, the judgment on the last day, heaven and hell, angels, Satan, and demons. This sounds much like Christianity, but the Muslims have a different definition and understanding of these beliefs.

Their clarification of these fundamentals is what separates the Christian from the Muslim.

The five pillars of Islam are the basis of the Muslim religion.

1. The confession of faith: There is only one god Allah and Muhammad is his prophet.
2. Prayers: Muslims are instructed to bow toward Mecca and pray five times daily. They are called to pray at designated times in the Arabic language.
3. Fasting: During the month of Ramadan, Muslims fast from sunrise to sunset. This is a time of meditation and prayer.
4. Pilgrimage: Muslims are to journey to Mecca at least once during their lives.
5. Almsgiving: Muslims are to tithe 2½ percent of their annual income to charity and the needs of society.

In the Qur'an, Christians are known as followers of "the Book." Because the Islamic religion does believe in some of the truths of the Bible, portions have been reworded according to Muhammad's interpretation. "I am only a human like you, revealed to me is that your God is One God" (surah 41:6).

To the Muslim, Allah is the one and only absolute one. Christians believe in the Trinity: Father, Son, and Holy Spirit. The greatest sin a Muslim can commit is *shirk,* to give God more than one property or position, which is blasphemy to Allah. "They do blaspheme who say Allah is one of three in a Trinity: for there is no god except One Allah. If they desist not from their word (of blasphemy), verily a grievous penalty will befall the blasphemers among them" (surah 5:73).

The Muslim believes Jesus was a mere man, a prophet from Allah. Allah would not lower himself to take a son. "And it [the

Qur'an] warns those who say: 'Allah has taken a son.' Surely, of this they have no knowledge, neither they nor their fathers; it is a monstrous word that comes from their mouths, they say nothing but a lie" (surah 18:4–5).

"O People of the Book! Commit no excesses in your religion: Nor say of God aught but the truth. Christ Jesus the son of Mary was (no more than) an apostle of God, and His Word, which He bestowed on Mary, and a spirit proceeding from Him: so believe in God and His apostles. Say not 'Trinity': desist: it will be better for you: for God is one God: Glory be to Him: (far exalted is He) above having a son. To Him belong all things in the heavens and on earth. And enough is God as a Disposer of affairs" (surah 4:171).

The Muslim does not believe in Christ's death and resurrection. "That they said (in boast), 'We killed Christ Jesus the son of Mary, the Apostle of God'- but they killed him not, nor crucified him, but so it was made to appear to them, and those who differ therein are full of doubts, with no (certain) knowledge, but only conjecture to follow, for of a surety they killed him not" (surah 4:157).

The Muslim believes his entrance into heaven is based on his good deeds outweighing the bad. "He forgiveth whom He pleaseth, and punisheth whom He pleaseth, for Allah hath power over all things" (surah 2:284). "For those things, that are good remove those that are evil" (surah 11:114).

The Muslim has an assurance of paradise only through the jihad. This can be a spiritual struggle or a holy war against the unbeliever. "And if ye are slain, or die, in the way of Allah, forgiveness and mercy from Allah are far better than all they could amass" (surah 3:157).

This doctrine of Islamic beliefs has profoundly impacted Sudan and the Lost Boys, particularly in the doctrine of jihad. In the case of the Lost Boys and their families, their faith has been forbidden by the government of Sudan. The southern people's stand to disobey the government's mandates to follow Islam has been one of the basic reasons that Khartoum has declared a jihad against southern Sudan. The Qur'an has definite instructions concerning those who refuse the Muslim faith.

"I will instill terror into the hearts of the Unbelievers: smite ye above their necks and smite all their finger-tips off them" (surah 8:12).

"Then fight and slay the Pagans wherever ye find them, and seize them, beleaguer them, and lie in wait for them in every stratagem (of war); but if they repent, and establish regular prayers and practice regular charity, then open the way for them: for Allah is Oft-forgiving, Most Merciful" (surah 9:5).

"Fight those who believe not in Allah nor the Last Day, who do not forbid what Allah and His Messenger have forbidden, and do not embrace the religion of the truth, being among those who have been given the Book, until they pay tribute out of the hand and have been humiliated" (surah 9:29).

"O Prophet, urge the believers to fight. If there are twenty patient men among you, you shall overcome two hundred, and if there are a hundred, they shall overcome a thousand unbelievers, for they are a nation who do not understand" (surah 8:65).

To many Muslims, acts of terrorism and persecution are justified in spreading their religion. To them, the struggle is noble, for Allah commands it. If the Muslim dies in the midst of fighting the infidel, the unbeliever of Islam, he believes he is immediately escorted to paradise. "Let those fight in the cause of Allah who sell the life of this world for the hereafter. To him who fighteth in the

cause of Allah—whether he is slain or gets victory—Soon shall
We give him a reward of great (value)" (surah 4:74).

Sano Masua, a Lost Boy, states, "I came to the United States
because I was told to convert to Islamic religion. I refused and told
them that I was born a Christian and I will die a Christian. If all
the riches of the world are to be all mine if I convert to Islam, then
I better be the poor of the poorest. For the kingdom of God will be
awaiting me. I really feel that I am blessed by coming here and at
the same time, I can work to help out of the situation [Sudan]."

Christian Doctrine

Christians believe in one God, who is Father, Son, and Holy
Spirit. He is a God of love, mercy, and compassion. He is the
Creator of the universe. God desires all mankind to follow Him
and to put their faith and trust in His Son, Jesus Christ. Jesus,
who is both God and man, is free from sin and willingly died on
a cross for our sins. Those who believe in His suffering, death,
and resurrection will one day live with Him in heaven.

Abraham, his brothers, and thousands of other Sudanese have
experienced firsthand persecution for their faith in God. They've
known and loved Christian martyrs and are prepared to die for
Jesus Christ.

The following information was gathered from *Unveiling
Islam* by Dr. Ergun Mehmet Caner and Dr. Emir Rethi Caner.

"'For God loved the world in this way: He gave His One and
Only Son, so that everyone who believes in Him will not perish
but have eternal life. For God did not send His Son into the
world that He might condemn the world, but that the world
might be saved through Him'" (John 3:16–17).

"In Him we have redemption through His blood, the forgiveness of our trespasses, according to the riches of His grace" (Eph. 1:7).

The Christian life allows choice within biblical guidelines. By God's grace our sins are forgiven—not through anything man may do but through faith in His Son. "For by grace you are saved through faith, and this is not from yourselves; it is God's gift" (Eph. 2:8). "Tell them: 'As I live'—the declaration of the Lord God—'I take no pleasure in the death of the wicked, but rather that the wicked person should turn from his way and live. Repent, repent of your evil ways! Why will you die, house of Israel?'" (Ezek. 33:11).

Christians believe in the right to worship freely. "First of all, then, I urge that petitions, prayers, intercessions, and thanksgivings be made for everyone, for kings and all those who are in authority, so that we may lead a tranquil and quiet life in all godliness and dignity" (1 Tim. 2:1–2). "Conduct yourselves honorably among the Gentiles, so that in a case where they speak against you as those who do evil, they may, by observing your good works, glorify God in a day of visitation. Submit to every human institution because of the Lord, whether to the Emperor as the supreme authority, or to governors as those sent out by him to punish those who do evil and to praise those who do good. For it is God's will that you, by doing good, silence the ignorance of foolish people. As God's slaves, [live] as free people, but don't use your freedom as a way to conceal evil. Honor everyone. Love the brotherhood. Fear God. Honor the Emperor" (1 Pet. 2:12–17).

Christians believe in spreading the truth of the Bible through preaching, teaching, lifestyle, and love in accordance with the instructions and example of Jesus Christ: "As you go, announce this: 'The kingdom of heaven has come near'" (Matt. 10:7). "Go, therefore, and make disciples of all nations, baptizing them in the name of the Father and of the Son and of the Holy Spirit" (Matt. 28:19). "Jesus said to them again, 'Peace to you! As the Father has sent Me, I also send you'" (John 20:21). "Now the Scripture says, **No one who believes on Him will be put to shame,** for there is no distinction between Jew and Greek, since the same Lord of all is rich to all who call on Him. For **everyone who calls on the name of the Lord will be saved**" (Rom. 10:11–13).

Jesus commands us Christians to love our enemies, to bless those who persecute us for our relationship with Him, and to respect all people. Love of God, His Son Jesus, and the Holy Spirit is to rule the Christian's every thought, word, and deed. "You have heard that it was said, **Love your neighbor** and hate your enemy. But I tell you, love your enemies and pray for those who persecute you, so that you may be sons of your Father in heaven. For He causes His sun to rise on the evil and the good, and sends rain on the righteous and the unrighteous" (Matt. 5:43–45). "But love your enemies, do [what is] good, and lend, expecting nothing in return. Then your reward will be great, and you will be sons of the Most High. For He is gracious to the ungrateful and evil. Be merciful, just as your Father also is merciful" (Luke 6:35–36).[1]

Abraham Nhial and his Sudanese brothers have seen the result of what happens to a country when its leaders do not serve the one, true, and living God but instead react in hatred to those who do not share in their beliefs. "Now the works of the flesh are obvious: sexual immorality, moral impurity, promiscuity, idolatry, sorcery, hatreds, strife, jealousy, outbursts of anger, selfish ambitions, dissensions, factions, envy, drunkenness, carousing, and anything similar, about which I tell you in advance—as I told you before—that those who practice such things will not inherit the kingdom of God" (Gal. 5:19–21).

How are the Lost Boys, with their commitment to Christ, supposed to respond to war? For that matter, how are Christians worldwide to respond to the militant Islamic regime of Sudan? These questions have been asked by Christians for centuries. The Bible neither permits nor prohibits war. "Everyone must submit to the governing authorities, for there is no authority except from God, and those that exist are instituted by God. So then, the one who resists the authority is opposing God's command, and those who oppose it will bring judgment on themselves. For rulers are not a terror to good conduct, but to bad" (Rom. 13:1–3).

Other biblical references state: "'No one has greater love than this, that someone would lay down his life for his friends'" (John 15:13). "'You are going to hear of wars and rumors of wars. See that you are not alarmed, because these things must take place, but the end is not yet. For nation will rise up against nation, and kingdom against kingdom. There will be famines and earthquakes in various places'" (Matt. 24:6–7).

Perhaps the second greatest commandment of all illuminates the matter. "'**Love your neighbor as yourself**'" (Matt. 22:39).

The boundaries separating Islam and Christianity focus on a personal relationship with God the Father, His Son Jesus Christ, and His Holy Spirit. The Person of God does not coincide with the Muslim ideal of Allah.

Christians believe in freedom of worship—in choice. God does not want puppets to maneuver at His whim; He desires a total abandonment to Him, a conscious decision made from the individual's free will.

The U.S. Department of State has listed Sudan as one of several countries that denies religious freedom.

Abraham is assured through God's promises that He is in the midst of Sudan's civil strife. God is with His people, encouraging and strengthening them through their many trials and persecutions. Nowhere in God's Word does He grant permission to wage war against innocent civilians, to imprison them, to torture or maim them, to deprive them of their families, food, homes, and medical care in order for them to change their way of life.

According to Kerby Anderson of Probe Ministries, there are essentially three Christian views concerning war.

1. Activism: It is always right to participate in war.
2. Pacifism: It is never right to participate in war.
3. Selectivism: It is right to participate in some wars.

Most Christians generally hold to the third position. This led to the development of what has come to be known as the just war criteria. A just war would include the following elements:

1. Just cause (defensive war)
2. Last resort (negotiations have failed)
3. Formal declaration
4. Limited objectives (the goal should be restoration of peace)
5. Proportionate means
6. Noncombatant immunity[2]

Abraham and the Lost Boys believe southern Sudan, through the SPLA, is fighting back to preserve the rights of the Christians and non-Christians who have suffered in this war. The southern

Sudanese will worship God regardless of the oppression. They know the pain of having airlifted food and medicine confiscated by the northern military. They've seen the results of strategically placed landmines where gardens once flourished. They've heard their children cry out for water when their wells have been filled with dirt and debris. Churches, schools, and hospitals are also destroyed when bombs destroy homes. Men, women, children, and soldiers are on their knees pleading for God's help.

The reality is people are dying every day, and the government is still bombing and killing people for the oil. The GOS doesn't care. They don't feel the pain and suffering. They don't respect human rights, and from my own experience, the GOS needs the land not the people.

ABRAHAM NHIAL

Chapter Eight

Rich Resources of the South

Abraham and his brothers have seen the trials of a failing economy, and they have faced the prejudice of two distinctly different cultures and races. Their plight began as a result of a Muslim government's commitment to forcing others to submit to Islam, and they experienced the ongoing struggle over the rich oil fields of the south.

Through the vast Sudan snakes the Nile River. This great, winding waterway runs south to north. The White Nile and the Blue Nile, the two main branches, join at Khartoum. The Lol River is a tributary of the White Nile. Without water, southern Sudan would be much like the large areas of the north—a vast desert region.

One railroad, usually controlled by the government, connects the north and south. Substantial transportation improvements are needed in the way of railroads, roads, and airports for the south to utilize its rich resources.

Sudan is one of the twenty-five poorest countries in the world. Eighty percent of the population works in agriculture with most of the farms used for individual or family needs. The country imports food, petroleum products, machinery, medicines, chemicals, and manufactured goods. Sudan is the largest exporter of gum arabic, made from the resin of the acacia tree. It grows in the northern areas of Sennar and Kordofan, and the substance is used in cooking, adhesives, and drugs. Other export products are cotton, sorghum, and oilseeds. Currently, Sudan's imports far exceed its exports. This deficit creates an enormous national debt, which is not being repaid.

Oil, the most lucrative resource in Sudan, is found predominantly in the south. The GOS is desperately seeking ways to fund the civil war, and its solution is to control the southern oil. Khartoum spends an estimated $1 million a day to finance the ongoing war. This heavy financial burden propels the government to increase the drilling in the oil-rich regions by forcibly removing people from their homes and ensuring the land cannot provide an adequate living for those who attempt to return. This is called a scorched-earth policy.

The oil problem is complex. Both north and south are determined to keep these reserves for themselves. Due to the expectation that Sudan's future lies in its oil fields, the north will not allow the south to establish an independent nation or control its own resources. On the other hand, the south needs permission to pass through the north in order to transport its products to the rest of the world through Port Sudan on the Red Sea.

The National Islamic Front (NIF) is the political faction currently controlling the GOS. Alarming reports about genocide in the areas of oil reserves are not propaganda from a single force or organization directed against the NIF, but firsthand accountings from respected workers of benevolent organizations and various government officials committed to helping the civilians caught in the Sudanese civil war. Among these are UN special rapporteurs, Amnesty International, Human Rights Watch, and the Harker Mission.

An estimated eleven thousand people displaced from Block 5a (an oil-rich region in southern Sudan called Muglad Basin) settled in the SPLA-controlled village of Nhialdiu. The village was already swollen by Nuer people who had been driven south from the Heglig area in earlier years. On July 15, 2000, government militias attacked Nhialdiu, burning every hut except one and displacing the inhabitants. A local chief said that militias rounded up the elderly, put them in one hut, and burned them alive. He said some of the dead were also very young children, five of them his own children.[1]

Abraham and other Sudanese believe the GOS desires only the oil not the people. An increase in aerial warfare with helicopter gunships has paved the way for soldiers and armed horsemen to drive out civilians. The people are murdered or sold as slaves, women are brutally raped, homes are destroyed, crops are burned, and livestock are killed in order to free the area for drilling. Thousands of civilians are displaced. Additional reports reveal Khartoum uses the all-weather roads and airstrips constructed by the oil companies to further advance scorched-earth warfare in the oil-rich regions. Most roads in the south are impassable during the rainy season, but these new well-built roads allow the GOS year-round passage.

On June 15, 1999, the U.S. House of Representatives passed H.R. 75 "condemning the National Islamic Front (NIF) government for its genocidal war in southern Sudan, support for terrorism, and continued human rights violations, and for other purposes." The Senate also later ratified the resolution.

Not only is the GOS conducting a genocidal war against southern Sudan, but foreign entities are accused of indirectly participating in human rights violation by helping the GOS profit from oil.

In August 1999, the first crude oil from the Greater Nile Petroleum Operating Company began flowing through a thousand-mile pipeline that runs from the south to Port Sudan. Partners in the Greater Nile project are Talisman Energy of Canada (25 percent), Malaysia's state-owned Petronas (30 percent), and China National Petroleum Corporation (40 percent). Khartoum's state-owned Sudapet has a nominal 5 percent stake but receives more than 40 percent of revenues, which will eventually rise to 80 percent. These three foreign corporate entities send hundreds of millions of dollars annually to the Khartoum regime, which is spending close to $1 million per day on its war.[2]

In February 2001, a Canadian-based organization released "Human Security in Sudan," also known as the Harker Report. It cited Talisman Energy of Canada for violating human rights. As a result of the Harker Report, the U.S. government prohibited financial transactions with the Sudan Greater Nile Oil Project.

In October 2001, Gerhart Baum, a UN human rights investigator from Germany, reported that the situation in Sudan has become "a war for oil."[3]

On October 16, 2001, a combination of British and Canadian nongovernment human rights investigators released "Investigation into Oil Development, Conflict and Displacement in Western Upper Nile, Sudan," which linked the oil companies and Sudan with the past and present atrocities committed against civilians.

Also in 2001, the humanitarian group Christian Aid released "The Scorched Earth: Oil and War in Sudan," which discussed oil involvement in the violation of human rights, the banning of aid in the western Upper Nile region, the use of oil money to purchase weapons for Khartoum to use against the south, oil companies' declared ignorance of the mass murders, and British firms supplying pumps and equipment for oil production. These activities show distinct scorn for the Geneva Conferences and humanitarian law.

The GOS has often ignored efforts to bring aid to the southern people and denied access to humanitarian organizations. Without food, water, and medical assistance, more will die. Famine proves to be Khartoum's most effective method of attack. More than two million people have been killed and four million displaced in southern Sudan. Khartoum has chosen not to bomb the southern military rebels or their camps and supplies; rather, it concentrates on regions occupied by civilians. If the civilians held any hope of returning to their homes, the thoughts have been destroyed in the wake of the devastation. To date, an estimated 50 percent of the population in the western Upper Nile region has been killed.

"Nominally Khartoum is the government of Sudan. What Khartoum really governs are the country's military resources—and the choices of civilian targets. Their favorites are undefended villages, schools, hospitals, herds of cattle, refugee centers and emergency feeding stations. One attack on a school in the Nuba region killed fourteen young children as they began their English lesson book, 'Read with Us.'"[4]

On February 20, 2002, the United Nations reported that in the village of Bieh, located in Block 5a, while women and children waited for the UN World Food Program to deliver needed food and medicine, helicopter gunships opened heavy fire on thousands of civilians. Khartoum knew of the drop and approved it, only to use the opportunity to murder innocent and needy civilians.[5]

The American Anti-Slavery Group (AASG) in March 2002 declared it had evidence to support Talisman Energy of Canada was behind the ethnic cleansing process in the oil regions. An April 2002 report from Calgary, Alberta, stated that under the Rome Statute of the International Criminal Court Talisman Oil can be liable for the crimes violating human rights issues. In June 2002, Talisman was rumored to be planning to pull out of Sudan. Indications are Talisman's decision was based on the sharp criticisms from human rights and church organizations worldwide. In addition, many U.S. political groups have condemned Talisman's role in Sudan's oil.[6]

The CPMT, a U.S. group led by retired Army Brig. Gen. Charles H. Baumann whose expertise is in African affairs and peace-keeping, was established in October 2002. The team is located in Khartoum and Rumbrek and operates independently of the GOS and the SPLA/SPLM. The CPMT function is to investigate alleged attacks on civilians and report the facts. Currently, the team has twenty monitors and an aircraft to use in its investigations. This team investigates despite the oil companies' policies to conduct business as usual and the GOS denying access to war-torn areas.

U.S. Secretary of State Colin Powell has said, "This is not the time to take the pressure off and especially to make sure that we keep a UN special rapporteur in place for Sudan."[7]

After Gerhart Baum made two trips for the United Nations to Sudan in October 2002 and February/March 2003, he reported that the civilians whose homes and villages were destroyed to make way for oil development had yet to benefit from the cease-fire. His report claimed that from December 2002 until February 2003, the GOS continued attacks on the civilians in the south. He saw no improvement in the human rights situation.

The situation in Sudan remains critical. Continued reports of ethnic cleansing by the government in the Darfur region have increased. Activists are urging war-crime tribunals. Human rights organizations worldwide are crying out for action for the atrocities against the civilians.

According to the *New York Times*, "(Darfur) is not a case when we can claim, as the world did after the Armenian, Jewish and Cambodian genocides, that we didn't know how bad it was. Sudan's refugees tell of mass killings and rapes, of women branded, of children killed, of villages burned—yet Sudan's government just stiffed new peace talks that began last night in Chad."[8]

The lines deepen on Abraham's face as he recounts the situation in the oil-rich area of his homeland. "The cry goes out to the rest of the world. This is inhumane. If we don't want this to continue, then we need mediators to bring the people together."

While the rest of the world believes in the peace talks, civilians are still being killed and displaced in the oil-rich regions. It is no wonder that many of the people of southern Sudan have lost hope in the free world coming to their aid. Many believe that while Sudanese President Omar al-Bashir states a peace agreement is close, he means the NIF will continue to use aggression to seek its goals. When the southern Sudanese do not see the former peace treaties making an impact on their lives, then they have little to believe in for future talks. Only time will tell.

At the close of World War II, North America and many European countries committed to a world free of genocide. Six million Jews gave their lives for the sake of ethnic cleansing. At how many deaths will the free world finally open its eyes to the murdered civilians in Sudan?

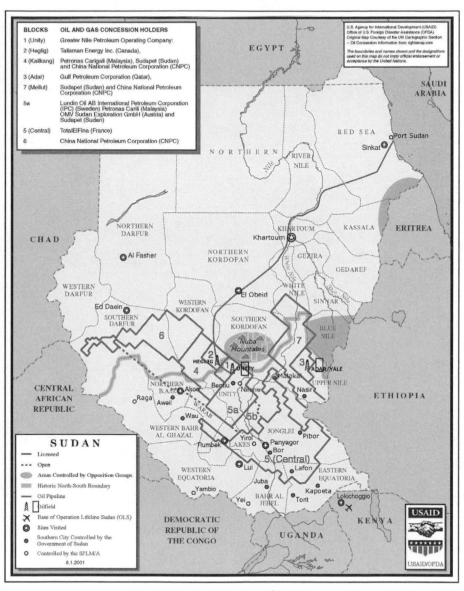

Map courtesy of USAID, www.usaid.gov; used with permission.

"This is what the LORD, the God of Israel, says: 'Let My people go.'"
EXODUS 5:1

Chapter Nine

Centuries of Slavery

When Abraham returned to his village in 1999, he learned about relatives who had been taken as slaves to north Sudan. The thought both saddened and angered him. Most of the free world today has no concept of the slavery existing in developing countries. Humanitarian and government organizations across the globe are working to end this inhumane practice.

For hundreds of years, Arab slave traders have raided southern Sudan, capturing black Africans—men, women, and children—for the purpose of selling them into servitude. In the past two decades, northern soldiers and slave traders have focused their attention on capturing women and children after the men of southern villages have been murdered.

"Sudan is one of the few countries in the world where slavery is currently a reality. Sudan's independence in 1956 did not stop the practice," Abraham states. His eyes tell the haunting story of those who have experienced the pain of losing loved ones to slavery. "Our country is still experiencing the ravages of civil war with more than an estimated two million deaths, the destruction of homes, crops, and livestock, and the displacement of thousands of refugees."

Those held in bondage are often denied food, clothing, shelter, and medical attention and are sexually abused and sometimes killed. One of the tribes affected by the slave raids is the Dinkas who live in the region known as Bahr al-Ghazal, especially the towns of Gogrial and Awiel where Abraham was born. As stated earlier, this region was home to the Lost Boys, where they not only lost loved and respected male members from their villages but also mothers, sisters, and other cherished women.

The Geneva Conferences and the United Nations along with various church and humanitarian organizations around the world have condemned the buying and selling of humans, but it has not stopped the practice going on today in Sudan. To deny slavery exists in war-torn Sudan allows it to continue. Those who ignore this situation are as much to blame as the slave traders who buy and sell innocent civilians for forced labor.

Many believe the Dinkas are targeted because of their heavy involvement in the SPLA/SPLM. Reports indicate the GOS is backing the Islamic movement to enslave these people. Raiding the civilian villages and carrying off the women and children into slavery, who are often families and friends of the SPLA military, cuts at the heart of those fighting to free Sudan from Khartoum's oppression. The government would like to think slavery dissuades the SPLA/SPLM, but instead it has made the southern guerrilla army stronger and more determined to push the northern regime from their land.

In the past, the raiding was accomplished during the dry season when the roads were passable, but since the oil companies have constructed all-weather roads, the practice extends into the rainy season. Reports indicate that with improved passageways the Sudanese government is offering incentives to those who desire to acquire slaves year around.

In the mid-1980s, two professors from the University of Khartoum, Ushari Ahmad Mahmud and Suleyman Ali Baldo, learned about the inhumane treatment aimed at the Dinka people. They delved into a fact-finding mission and discovered the government instigated the murdering of the men and the capturing of the women and children as slaves. Mahmud and Ali Baldo released a written report in 1987, which the government termed false. The two professors were jailed, and Khartoum then set out to destroy their credibility. UN representatives later rejected Mahmud and Suleyman's document as unreliable.

As the genocide and slavery persisted, Sudanese Catholic, Presbyterian, and Episcopalian church officials pushed forward with the same reports of mass murders and slavery of the Dinkas. Currently, one can purchase a slave for approximately thirty-five dollars, sometimes for fifty to ninety-five dollars. The Arabs need slaves to work in their communities and in the fields, making the business profitable for the traders while the government denies the practice. It's been reported that girls, as young as eight years old, are used for sexual pleasures and are often sexually mutilated. Violence against women is common in the war-torn areas. It is estimated that 80 percent of the civilians killed in the civil war have been women.[1]

The enslaved children are indoctrinated into Islam and given Islamic names. They are forbidden to use their Christian or tribal names. All children in Sudan are refused an education unless they have completed two years' instruction of the Qur'an. Many of the boys are placed in camps where they are severely beaten and forced to learn the Muslim religion, then later forced to serve in the GOS military.

Whether a woman is a slave or simply living under Islamic law, she does not have the rights of a man. Women are often beaten severely for not adhering to dress codes and speaking out against the discrimination and degradation of their country's policies. Women slaves suffer cruel and appalling treatment inconceivable by the free world.

Christians are arrested, tortured, and enslaved for their faith. They are thrown into jail and denied communication with friends and family. It has been reported that a Christian can expect forty lashes for taking communion. Family members are often killed in an effort to stop the spread of Christianity.

Under President Clinton's administration, Secretary of State for African Affairs Susan Rice visited Sudan and reported on the atrocities committed against the people there, confirming the reports of human rights violations, scorched-earth policy, and slavery.

Through the work of Christian Solidarity International (CSI), headquartered in Zurich, Switzerland, thousands of slaves have been redeemed since 1995. Prior to this time, in the 1980s, the African chiefs funded the release price of slaves through Arab go-betweens. Since then, the redemption price has received international financial support from private individuals and benevolent organizations alleviating the burden from friends and family of the slaves.

Lucian Niemeyer, a CSI worker in Sudan, gave the following report on slavery:

A young boy of eight was captured in a raid. While walking to the masters' homes a young girl could not walk further and collapsed. The Arabs cut her head off, killing her immediately. They told the young boy to carry the head. For five days the boy carried the head. By this time the head was disintegrating and was so smelly that the captors told him to burn it. In the Dinka tradition, burning any human body parts was taboo. An older woman nearby raised her hands and voice in protest. She was severely beaten. Then the captors put a gun to the head of the boy, and he burned the head. That was six years ago. The memory was evidently fresh as if it was today, in his mind.

I heard so many stories like this one. A girl resisting rape had her hand placed into a bed of hot coals causing her fingers to be burned off. Then the five captors each had their way with her. Another very pretty girl had her captors get into a fight over her. Each wanted her for his wife. After a severe fight they stopped, determining that she was the cause. They placed hot knife points to her chest and burned it severely. It was one episode after another. The cruelty of the northern Muslims on the Christian Dinkas, whom they considered unclean and an inferior people, is uniquely sadistic and cruel. Today, 707 slaves were redeemed.[2]

Friendly Arabs locate lost members of the affected families and take them to a designated area to redeem. Missions to emancipate these slaves are perilous. The flight into Sudan and the danger of being shot down by the government is an ever-present risk. Landing strips are nothing more than dirt roads where cattle and goats roam. No luxury hotels or five-star restaurants greet the redeemers, only the faces of those willing to offer their hospitality, and in some cases the SPLA guards in the event of attack.

Southern Sudanese share the same hope: liberate the slaves, stop the genocide, and permit freedom of worship. The Dinkas and other African tribes have existed for hundreds of years as a pastoral people; a tranquil lifestyle is what they desperately crave. The peaceful past is what motivates them, woven with a profound faith in a God who is in control and hears their prayers.

Niemeyer also related this story: "Some two weeks after I was there, Marial Bai, a village where we redeemed slaves and met with the Anglican bishop of Wau, was attacked and destroyed. More than one hundred women and children were taken, as well as livestock. Five Dinka men followed the north-bound column attempting to recover their wives and children. They were discovered and their arms were cut off at the shoulders and they were left to die. Three men did die from the loss of blood and two survived. They were airlifted by CSI to Nairobi, where to the best of my knowledge, they are recovering. Maybe it was in retribution for our visit. Surely, the cruelty and the genocide does not stop."[3]

Human rights organizations have repeatedly appealed to Khartoum to assist families who search for their loved ones, but to date little has been accomplished. The GOS continues to claim slavery is prohibited and the humanitarian accusations are false. Various reports from humanitarian organizations indicate the number of southern Sudanese held against their will is difficult to determine, but several thousand is a good indication. Khartoum claims the criticisms are an internal problem existing between hostile African tribes, and the situations are impossible to control because of the remote locations of the southern people. In addition, the government fails to assist those who are victimized. In the Sudan Criminal Code of 1991, slavery is not barred, but the government has given formal sanction to many international treaties that prohibit slavery.

In April 1996, the UN special representative for the Sudan alarmed the world with its reports of slavery and forced labor. Previously, the UN adopted a resolution that human rights violations were world crimes, but the general consensus was the world should work with Khartoum in improving the situation in the south, not inflame tensions against it.

In June of 1996, two reporters from the *Baltimore Sun* unlawfully entered Sudan. They purchased two slaves and later freed them. Their series of articles, titled "Witness to Slavery," attracted worldwide attention.

Julia Aker Duany, founder of SSFI, describes what she found in a Sudanese camp: "Some of the African refugees are held in large camps in the desert outside of the northern towns. In 1993, I slipped into one of the worst refugee camps near Khartoum. I had to disguise myself and dress in rags because the guards will not allow outsiders to enter the camp. While I was inside this camp, I noticed some healthy-looking children who were kept segregated from the rest and given better food. I was sickened to learn that these African children and others like them in other camps are northern Sudan's living blood bank. Every two weeks, a measure of their blood is taken and given to casualties among the northern soldiers."[4]

In 1999, through the efforts of Unicef and other benevolent organizations and embassies, the Committee for the Eradication of the Abduction of Women and Children (CEAWC) was formed. This committee comprised Dinka representatives and James Agware, a Dinka living in Khartoum who had actively pursued the releasing of slaves since the mid-1980s. The CEAWC met in Khartoum to discuss the alleged slavery problem. As a result, the government of Sudan agreed to help women and children find their families and homes. The CEAWC was successful in liberating hundreds of slaves. Those who did not find their families were returned to Khartoum and educated in the Muslim schools and universities.

In 1999 and again in 2001, the GOS declared it would arrest and prosecute those involved with slavery and asked for the people to report missing family members and friends. However, no cases were ever brought to court.

On April 21, 2001, the United Nations condemned Sudan for violating human rights but did not, however, specifically denounce Sudan's slavery practices.

In December 2001, John Danforth, the U.S. special envoy for peace in Sudan, announced the GOS and the SPLA had agreed to work together in an effort to end the slavery issue. Secretary of State Powell appointed Penn Kemble, senior scholar at Freedom House, to investigate and make recommendations concerning slavery to an international group. As of this writing, nothing has been resolved.

Since 1995, humanitarian and church organizations outside

of Sudan have worked to buy back or redeem slaves for their families. Because of this highly publicized endeavor, critics have released their findings for and against the redemption process.

Arguments against Slave Redemption

Periodically, the hostile tribes of southern Sudan have agreed to stop raiding in exchange for water or grazing areas for their cattle. Various reports indicate this has angered the GOS, and it has initiated incentives to continue the slave raids.

Since the SPLA began providing weapons for the boys guarding cattle in the areas prone to slave raids, the number of incidents may have actually decreased. Before this, the civilians had no defense against their abductors. Critics of this practice state that arming boys promotes child soldiers, but in actuality it is a viable way to protect villages from the raids.

No one has been able to keep an accurate account of how many civilians have been captured as slaves. With the attacks from Khartoum, displacement of families, famine, drought, and low literacy, the names and numbers of those missing are impossible to estimate.

Fraud constitutes a major concern in the value of slave redemption. Middlemen, seeking to fill their pockets, act as dealers to those seeking to redeem loved ones. Women and children are borrowed or rented to increase the size of the slave population and increase the middlemen's profits. To halt this money-making venture, a private group has stepped forward to take accurate accountings from those who are searching for family members. Its goal is to produce a list of names, dates of abductions, and descriptions of the captured to ensure the alleged slaves are actually redeemable.

Early in 1999, critics of the SPLA reported that members of the guerrilla army posed as Arab traders to make money redeeming slaves. For all the reasons cited, Human Rights Watch opposes slave redemption. It believes all those who are involved in raiding for slaves and selling them should be prosecuted.

The following is the viewpoint of a Lost Boy: "Slavery is an immoral device against humanity. In my own view, slave redemption is not the right answer to eradicate this unlawful practice. However, it is a relief to people who have been caught up in the crossfire. If you are guided by the market theory of supply and demand to argue redemption of slaves, you may misinterpret the real cause of Sudanese slavery. This kind of market [Sudan government] is not guided by the market rules. Here the market has a political motivation rather than a market incentive. People of the south have refused to accept Islamic culture as well as the language and religion since the fall of the Christian kingdom at the end of the medieval era."

This particular Lost Boy wishes to remain anonymous, but he does believe that slavery is the government's means of converting southern Sudanese to Islam. He continues, "The best way to destroy slavery is to change the regime in Sudan."

In conclusion, those who argue against slave redemption believe refusing to pay the redemption price reduces the profit lure of the slave trade.

Arguments for Slave Redemption

Many humanitarian and church organizations as well as private individuals are shocked and outraged at the idea of slavery existing in the world today. They advocate doing whatever is nec-

essary to free innocent victims. Story after story of those beaten
and persecuted by their abductors moves them to pay the price to
return slaves to their families. Some have seen firsthand the tear-
ful reunions, a slave's fear of rejection by his or her family, women
who now have children fathered by their abductors, and those
who have aged years with the suffering. Any cost, including lin-
ing the pockets of the middlemen, is worth paying to redeem
slaves.

Whether a Christian or a champion for those denied their
human rights, there will always be advocates who are willing to
risk their lives and find the funds to free slaves.

Arguments for and against slave redemption in Sudan have
two goals in mind: to free all the slaves in Sudan and to end the
practice. Only through the commitment and actions of
Khartoum to end slavery and punish slave traders and the dili-
gent, involved efforts of international and national humanitarian
organizations can slavery effectively be abolished.

Abraham speaks about his cousins who were captured by
northern soldiers. "They were little boys abducted by the enemy
when their village was attacked and I fled my home. No one
knows what happened to them, but we assume they are now
slaves somewhere in northern Sudan. I met young ladies and boys
who had been slaves but were freed because Americans had paid
for them to be free.

"The fact is, collecting money to free slaves may encourage
the slave traders to take more of the people, and they are making
money, but it does free some of the people. It also lets the rest of
the world know slavery is in our country. In other words, if we
don't free them, how will the rest of the world know about this

horrible custom? The reality is, slavery is practiced no matter if the government denies it. How are we going to free these people? I have to believe that slave redemption is the only way until there is peace in Sudan. The suffering continues. Peace is desperately needed as we [the Lost Boys] have been sharing with the Americans and the rest of the world."

Abraham reports that Francis Bok, a former slave boy who now lives in the United States and is a part of an antislavery board in southern Sudan, works to obtain assistance from the United States to help free slaves.

"I would like to encourage all the body of Christ to pray for peace," Abraham pleads. "I'm also encouraging all the leaders of the world to live in peace and to reach out to those people they are leading—not to benefit themselves but those they are leading. Ignoring the oppression and slavery in our country will not bring it to an end. We all encourage Americans to write their congressmen to help us stop slavery by demanding peace."

I worry about the people in Kakuma constantly.
I want so much for them, but I am one man,
but we have God who can do anything.

ABRAHAM NHIAL

Chapter Ten

Kakuma Today

The refugee camp in Kakuma was established in 1991 under the jurisdiction of the UNHCR. It is located seventy-five miles south of Sudan in a desolate area that does not promote vegetation. Currently it houses approximately ninety thousand displaced persons from Sudan, Burundi, Eritrea, Ethiopia, Democratic Republic of Congo, Rwanda, Somalia, and Uganda. Sudanese are 70 percent of the population. The UNHCR supports the camp along with the assistance of nongovernmental organizations. The IRC, LWF, Action by Churches Together (ACT), the Episcopal Church, Red Cross, Samaritan's Purse, Persecution Project, Voice of the Martyrs, Safe Harbor, Servants Heart, Sudan Interior Mission (SIM), and others share the many responsibilities of caring for the large refugee community.

The Lost Boys in Kakuma are the future of Sudan. They are intelligent and eager to learn about the world. Their survival before arriving at the camp with the overwhelming odds against them proves this point. They are now in their twenties, possess a teachable spirit, and have a humble spirit, broken and open to Christ. Education still remains their key focus.

In June 2002, Frank Blackwood, director of Aid Sudan Foundation in Houston, and his wife Debbie joined a team of ten volunteers on a mission of love and mercy to Kakuma and in Sudan. The team had four objectives in southern Sudan but accomplished eight objectives while there.

1. Dr. Richard Bransford, director of the Bethany Crippled Children's Hospital in Kijabe, Kenya, set up a medical clinic and treated more than two hundred people. Most were children suffering from a fatal disease called nodding disease. This disease does not have a known cause or cure and is always terminal.

2. Fifty letters were delivered from the Lost Boys in Houston to the Lost Boys in Kakuma.

3. Frank and Debbie visited the schools in Kakuma that served the refugees. They were able to meet with the headmaster and many of the students.

4. The team met with Koffi Mable, the director of Kakuma, and discussed the situation of the Lost Boys and Lost Girls in the refugee camp. They addressed current needs and made observations about community needs and critical issues.

5. Frank and Debbie traveled to southern Sudan and helped rebuild a bombed school.

6. Frank pulled a 120-foot pipe that was full of rust and dirt from a water well, cleaned the well, and replaced the pipe.

7. The *Jesus* film was shown to an entire village in the native language. These people had never seen a film before. Many accepted Christ, including the chief of the village.

8. Team members established a rebuilding program in the village where the film was shown. The village is now called the Genesis Project. The program calls for building a compound that will include a church, school, housing for teachers and ministers, and lodging for mission teams to come in the future to help in the redevelopment of the area.

During the 2002 mission trip, Blackwood told the Lost Boys that the people in the United States loved them because they worked hard, attended school, participated in church, and were not getting into trouble. The Lost Boys in the United States had not forgotten their friends and family left behind in Kakuma. In turn, the Sudanese community was encouraged to hear American Christians had taken their future leaders under their wings to disciple, mentor, and help educate them. The survivors are among the brightest and best of Sudan's people, the leaders of tomorrow.

In June 2003, Abraham Nhial accompanied twenty volunteers from Houston to Kakuma on a mission trip. Most of the members of the team were lay people, eager to learn more about Sudan and to help in any way possible—not only in ministry but also in any area that contributes to the welfare of the people. Frank Blackwood and Dr. William D. Boyd, president of the College of Biblical Studies in Houston, were among the team members, as well as two high school teachers.

As an active board member of the Aid Sudan Foundation, Abraham had personal and other goals for the trip. His personal goals were to get married, to see his father, to visit with the people of Kakuma, and to share the gospel of Jesus Christ. His ministry goals were to:

- Assist Dr. Boyd in training pastors.
- Help American volunteers see the life of a refugee. Through the volunteers' firsthand experiences and knowledge, others in the United States will see how the refugees are suffering. News travels most effectively by word of mouth.
- Bring one thousand letters and pictures from the Lost Boys in the United States to families, friends, and girlfriends in the refugee camp.

Frank Blackwood says, "The Lost Boys are easy to distinguish; the Lord has obviously handpicked and pruned them from nothing to His Providence. These people have the love of God about them—happy, talkative, with an anointing of the Lord."[1]

The Kakuma refugee camp is divided into eight zones; each zone is divided into groups. Each group contains people of the same nationality. For example, Zone Four/Group Two is a group of Somalian refugees. Abraham lived in Zone Six. The camp tries to keep different nationalities together. This gives the refugees a sense of unity among those of the same culture.

The Turkana people who live near Kakuma resent the refugee camp and the many occupants who have invaded their territory. Crime is a serious problem. To make matters worse, a five-year drought has affected the area, depleting the already limited resources. Bandits attack cattle herders and those traveling to and from the camp. Aid workers are also targeted in the rising hostility. To increase security, the camp has enlisted the aid of Kenyan

Kakuma Refugee Camp Zones

Map as of June 2002

UNHCR Regional Spatial Analysis Lab (RSAL): Nairobi, Kenya

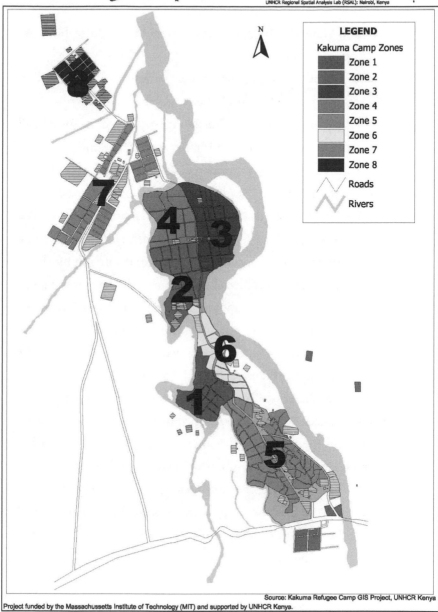

Source: Kakuma Refugee Camp GIS Project, UNHCR Kenya

Project funded by the Massachussetts Institute of Technology (MIT) and supported by UNHCR Kenya.

Map courtesy of ReliefWeb, www.reliefweb.int; used with permission.

police and trained refugee guards. Some of the Lost Boys are refugee guards.

The cost of sustaining the refugee camp is fourteen million dollars annually, which is funded entirely through contributions. The conditions are nearing the emergency stage as more and more refugees from Sudan and other persecuted peoples seek refuge. The camp must be prepared to house great numbers of people at any given hour and provide food, water, basic provisions, shelter, and sanitary conditions. A large majority of the refugees require medical attention. Most are children, who are often orphaned, followed by older women and nursing mothers.

Currently, the big problem in Kakuma is the lack of food and sanitary water. Due to the shortage of water, the wells are open for only a few hours a day. Refugees must fill their buckets then or do without. The refugees' daily water rations last until the middle of the night, then are gone.

For more than a decade, this camp has been home to thousands of refugees from neighboring countries. Provisions donated from around the world are intended to last fifteen days, but the allotment seldom extends the full period. Seventy percent of Kakuma's food supply comes from the United States, but it's not enough to avoid malnutrition. Various humanitarian organizations say the amount of food needed in Kakuma is at emergency levels. This is a bleak outlook for a refugee camp in existence for this long a time.

In January 2002, the camp was forced to drop a program that supplied school children with a daily feeding of porridge. This decline in nutrition will have an adverse effect on the overall quality of life, children's development, and lactating mothers. It will increase the possibility of starvation. Morale is low, which leads to desperate people attempting desperate means to survive. Many are plagued with the disease of hopelessness. Fighting and murders linked to depression are common.

The famine in Sudan and among refugees is of mammoth proportions. Among the humanitarian agencies striving to help the people are:

- Catholic Relief Services
- Care
- International Committee of the Red Cross
- International Rescue Committee
- Lutheran World Federation
- Medecins Sans Frontieres (Doctors Without Borders)
- Norwegian People's Aid
- Operation Lifeline Sudan
- Save the Children
- U.S. Committee for Refugees
- Unicef
- UN World Food Program
- World Vision

The IRC reports that the lack of food will eventually cost the donors more money than they are currently spending due to the medical costs incurred by the shortages. In addition, hostility and violence are increasing in a society deprived of basic food needs. Health issues are worsening causing a serious situation to become more critical.

"We received one meal a day which consisted of a starch mixture made from maize, provided by the UNHCR. It's tasteless but does contain nutrients to sustain life," Abraham says.

The food is rationed for a 1,600-calorie diet. This is the not the recommended 2,300 calories, but all that can be obtained with the limited donations. Unfortunately, the soil around the camp is not suitable for growing crops, which makes the community completely dependent on transported provisions from humanitarian organizations.

The refugee camp is an assortment of sights, sounds, smells, and tastes, under a sweltering sun. One hears a low hum during school hours, then the peals of laughter when the pupils—both young and old—are released for the day. The children are always ready for play. In the late afternoon, men and boys gather to play soccer. Cheers and shouts of encouragement soar above the thud of feet making contact with the ball. Near the water wells and medical clinic, different languages blend with the crowds of people, drawing the observer into the world of a refugee camp.

"I now live in Atlanta," Abraham says. "The heat here is bad during the summer, but the hot sun of Kakuma scorches the skin."

Red dirt blows continuously across the plains, mingling with the scrub brush and settling on everything including in people's mouths. For those whose hearts and minds are filled with sorrow and hopelessness, the environment does not help the downtrodden mentality.

Keeping peace in the camp requires careful planning of each day. Activities for all ages are scheduled to keep tensions low. Soccer and basketball utilize pent-up energy. Men and women learn crafts and develop skills they can use when they can return to their homeland or resettle in another country. Other than attending school, there is little else to occupy the refugees' time. Since there are no jobs to perform, the men who are heads of households are not able to fulfill their roles as providers. Their traditions and cultures are joys of the past. Perhaps the men are the most frustrated of all. Here, as in all parts of the world, a man's work is his life. Without it, he feels useless.

Living conditions are poor with the refugees living in cramped, slum-type conditions. Crude housing and improper sanitation cause disease and general discontent.

Education

Education is important to all Sudanese, especially in the ever-changing world. The tribal leaders strive to preserve their traditions and encourage education. They value the preservation of the past and want to offer a hopeful outlook for the future.

"We cannot compete with the rest of the world in the area of economics without educating our people," Abraham says. "It is the key to unlocking our future."

Education is the only way to help the refugees rise above the circumstances that have brought them to Kakuma. It's one of the highest priorities in the refugee community. Many of the Lost Boys call education their mother and father.

Patterned after the school system in Kenya, the educational programs are open to all the children, regardless of nationality. As of the writing of this book, those enrolled in Kakuma's schools total approximately twenty-nine thousand children, which is about 35 percent of the total population. Authorities state the education process is one of the major factors in establishing a peaceful existence among the different nationalities. English is the official language of Kenya and is taught and spoken in the camp schools.

Kakuma Refugee Camp Overview

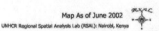

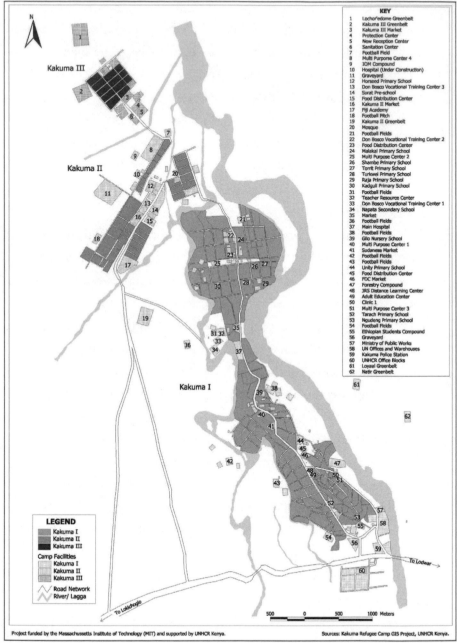

KEY

1. Lochor'edome Greenbelt
2. Kakuma III Greenbelt
3. Kakuma III Market
4. Protection Center
5. New Reception Center
6. Sanitation Center
7. Football Field
8. Multi Purpose Center 4
9. IOM Compound
10. Hospital (Under Construction)
11. Graveyard
12. Horseed Primary School
13. Don Bosco Vocational Training Center 3
14. Surat Pre-school
15. Food Distribution Center
16. Kakuma II Market
17. Fiji Academy
18. Football Pitch
19. Kakuma II Greenbelt
20. Mosque
21. Football Fields
22. Don Bosco Vocational Training Center 2
23. Food Distribution Center
24. Malakal Primary School
25. Multi Purpose Center 2
26. Shambe Primary School
27. Torrit Primary School
28. Turkwel Primary School
29. Raja Primary School
30. Kadgull Primary School
31. Football Fields
32. Teacher Resource Center
33. Don Bosco Vocational Training Center 1
34. Napata Secondary School
35. Market
36. Football Fields
37. Main Hospital
38. Football Fields
39. Gilo Nursery School
40. Multi Purpose Center 1
41. Sudanese Market
42. Football Fields
43. Football Fields
44. Unity Primary School
45. Food Distribution Center
46. FDC Market
47. Forestry Compound
48. JRS Distance Learning Center
49. Adult Education Center
50. Clinic 1
51. Multi Purpose Center 3
52. Tarach Primary School
53. Ngudeng Primary School
54. Football Fields
55. Ethiopian Students Compound
56. Graveyard
57. Ministry of Public Works
58. UN Offices and Warehouses
59. Kakuma Police Station
60. UNHCR Office Blocks
61. Loyaal Greenbelt
62. Natir Greenbelt

LEGEND

- Kakuma I
- Kakuma II
- Kakuma III

Camp Facilities
- Kakuma I
- Kakuma II
- Kakuma III

/\ Road Network
/\/\ River/ Lagga

500 0 500 1000 Meters

Project funded by the Massachussetts Institute of Technology (MIT) and supported by UNHCR Kenya.

Sources: Kakuma Refugee Camp GIS Project, UNHCR Kenya.

Map courtesy of ReliefWeb, www.reliefweb.int; used with permission.

There are three levels of schools.

1. Six early childhood schools or preschools in which math, English, outdoor play, and Swahili are taught.

2. Twenty-four primary schools teach math, English, geography, history, civics, religion, science, Kiswahili (Swahili), art craft, home science, music, physical education, and peace education.

3. Three secondary or high schools teach math, English, biology, chemistry, physics, commerce, business education, geography, history, and government.

The students are not limited to high school but have the ability to advance in learning through the University of South Africa's distance learning program. Entrance into this university is based on school performance. A few undergraduate students are able to receive an advanced education in Kenya through private sponsors.

The IRC and LWF have worked together to implement a program of special education for children who are severely disabled. These disabilities range from the hearing impaired to the mentally challenged and are taught by teachers who have received additional training. A sign language program has begun at the primary level. The camp schools plan to establish more of these units in the future for the partially blind and those with lesser disabilities. This program will enable these children to successfully integrate into the regular schools.

Vocational training is a vital part of the education process for young and old. As of the writing of this book, approximately five hundred students are enrolled in various courses and trades—tailoring, carpentry, computer skills, typewriting, welding, and so forth.

Evans Mburu, the IRC adult education director at Kakuma, says, "The refugees come to the camp with different skills, which they teach others, regardless of ethnic background—tailoring, carpet weaving, carpentry, handloom weaving, embroidery, leatherwork, and crocheting. Persons with disabilities are given first priority. The training continues for a period of nine months after which the trainees are examined in their specific areas of training."[2]

Twelve educational professionals oversee the schools. The teachers are recruited from among the refugees and from those who are university trained. Most teachers are untrained but willing to learn and share their knowledge among the students. The community is encouraged to become directly involved with the school program. This experience enables the refugees to feel a part of the community, with the hope that one day they will share their information with others. It promotes self-management and a sense of pride in the betterment of the camp.

With many different cultures and ethnic groups living in close quarters, the refugees are practicing methods to coexist peaceably. The IRC and LWF have combined efforts to teach and train all those in the camp who express a desire to learn. More counselors, social workers, and trained teachers would enhance the quality of the refugees' lifestyle and better prepare them for the future.

As of December 2003, 3,492 Lost Boys who trekked across Sudan are now too old to qualify for the U.S. refugee program. Higher education would not only fill their idle hours but would fill their minds with what they can do when they return to their homeland.

In a report dated June 2002, from Jason Phillips, country director of IRC Kenya, is an appeal to the U.S. Senate to not only increase U.S. contributions to Kenya but also offer the refugees a better life. "The high malnutrition rate suggests that there are many vulnerable people in Kakuma who, under continuing poor or deteriorating general rations, stand to slide into a life-threatening situation," Phillips says.[3]

The grim situation in Kakuma has touched all of the refugees' lives. These people have experienced war, starvation, and genocide. They have few if any personal belongings and desperately need medical attention. Education is limited, and without proper schooling their opportunities for a brighter tomorrow are greatly reduced. With the lingering war, many have lost hope of ever returning to their homeland. Those who have been born in Kakuma or were young when they arrived have no concept of a real home. Worldwide donations are shrinking as the war on terrorism depletes available funds.

Even with the short supply of provisions, living in Kakuma is better than existing in Sudan where there are no guarantees of water, food, health facilities, or safety. Inside Sudan is an active war zone, which means the inhabitants encounter land mines and live with the constant threat of northern soldiers. Schools and hospitals are bombed, and the education system suffers from lack of qualified, full-time teachers. Because there is no money to pay the teachers, they must work half a week to earn money and teach half a week. School supplies are nil unless these are flown in. Good drinking water is difficult to find, which leads to many other diseases from the contaminated wells, rivers, and streams. Medical care is scarce, with one primitive hospital for every

500,000 people. War, famine, and poverty continue to plague them. Because they have nothing, the smallest ray of hope brings joy to these villages.

Abraham encourages the people of Kakuma to hold on to their faith in God. He is the strength that sustains them when they are at their weakest. Their children are sick and often hungry. They remember the atrocities committed in Sudan. They crave education. It has been said that the Lost Boys will work as hard for an education as they did when they walked more than one thousand miles to safety.

Southern Sudan, after twenty years of civil war, will not be rebuilt overnight. It will take many years to work out all the problems in peace-making efforts, but the work begins with the first step toward giving the Sudanese their dignity.

The following are feelings in verse from the refugees in Kakuma.

What Is a Refugee?
What is a refugee?
Well and good to answer,
To answer such a question, we need to be careful,
Because those who can answer it are very rare in this world.

To answer such a question
Needs you first to take refuge,
Otherwise your answer will be simple and meaningless.

As refugees,
We are victims of violence and war,
We left our motherland
Because we were being mistreated in many ways.
We ran to get protection in other countries.

But as a refugee,
You are always simple in front of anybody.
You are subject to prejudice and mistaken ways.
You are a human being without any value.
You can pass through any disaster
And nobody will care about you.

Oh, what is lovely like our homeland?
In your own country you are free,
Free like a butterfly when it flies from flower to flower,
Free like a fish moving in water.

Homeland is a second heaven,
Without your home
You are like a dog without a tail.

Give us peace,
To return to our beloved country,
Our precious heaven Sudan.
Give us our ancestors' land.

ANDREW MAYAK,
KAKUMA REFUGEE CAMP

Why Don't You Go Back?
Please don't ask me
"Why don't you go back?"
Do you think I like staying?
For twelve grains of beans.
Two week rations.
To stay without soap,
Suffering malaria and typhoid,
Here in the bush,
With wind, dust, blowing trumpet,
Where nature is playing
Its ugliest games.
Do you think I like staying?
Seeking second-hand clothes,

If I could help myself,
If I could rebuild my homeland.
Do you think I like staying?
Without my wife, husband, children,
My father, mother, sister, brother, family.
Without feeling homesick.

Please don't ask me
"Why don't you go back?"
Humans destroying each other,
Where human sense has lost its value,
War, tribal, religious conflicts,
Destroy peace, democracy,
Where there is war,
Where there is conflict,
Where there is fear and persecution,
Where there is no democracy,
Where human rights are violated,
I can't go back.
I am destined to suffer,
In Exile,
Until, I go back,
Until my time comes,
Until then, I will stay.

Please don't ask me
"Why don't you go back?"
I WOULD IF I COULD,
World humanitarian community:
Understand that
It's not simple or easy,
Avoiding past memory.
I CAN'T REMOVE FROM MY MIND,
My traditional culture, my sentimental torture,
My folktales of childhood,
Never old, never dead,
Stamped in my mind.

I have normal feelings,
I suffer for dignity
Please don't kill my broken heart,
By asking me
"Why don't you go back?"
I will if I can,
I wouldn't sit a moment,
When the new dawn comes.

YILMA TAFERE,
KAKUMA REFUGEE CAMP

The LORD will always lead you,
satisfy you in a parched land,
and strengthen your bones.
You will be like a watered garden
and like a spring whose waters never run dry.
Some of you will rebuild the ancient ruins;
you will restore the foundations laid long ago;
you will be called the repairer of broken walls,
the restorer of streets where people live.

ISAIAH 58:11–12

Chapter Eleven

The Church in Kakuma and Sudan

Abraham is proud of the Christian church in Sudan: "The history of the Sudanese church is a remarkable one, a wonderful reminder of the way God blesses His people even in the most difficult of circumstances."

Early Greek recordings show Nubian kings converted to Christianity around 540 when the Byzantine Empire sent missionaries to preach the gospel, although some writings indicate Christian missionaries present in the previous century. The book of Acts records the baptism of Queen Candace's minister, marking the first Christian Sudanese community in Meroë. Since its beginnings, the Sudanese church has struggled against those who sought to destroy it.

American Presbyterians and British Anglicans in the 1800s, with the Anglicans working primarily among the Dinka people, established churches throughout the south. The missionaries built churches, schools, and medical clinics to give the people a good quality of life not only spiritually but also mentally and physically. They trained the converts to lead and direct the people so the missionaries could move on to establish more Christian-led communities. In 1964 when the Muslim government took over, the Muslims tightened control of the Christian churches by using whatever tactics needed to dissuade the people from Christianity. Despite government opposition, the church continues to grow. The African Sudanese Christians suffer considerably for their faith, and yet they are eager to spread the gospel of Jesus Christ.

During the past two decades, as war rages through southern Sudan, the church has grown despite its opposition. Some reports indicate the church of Sudan has grown faster than any other church in the world.

"We, the Sudanese, feel the presence of God in our worship," Abraham says. "There is joy and happiness in the hearts of everyone. We share in the persecution of the church in southern Sudan and the Nuba Mountains because of our security in Jesus Christ. During our travels to Ethiopia, to Sudan, and to Kenya, we faced many difficulties and lost many people because we lacked that security. God who is love and who is unchanging and everlasting is our greatest eternal security. Those of us who believe in God's provisions understand He took care of us during the journey. It has been said, 'Persecution is the seed of the gospel.'"

The GOS's persecution through bombing churches and unexplained fires does not differentiate among denominations; it targets all Christians.

The Sudan Council of Churches (SCC) and the New Sudan Council of Churches (NSCC) include all those churches serving in northern and southern Sudan. They include Catholic, Orthodox, and Protestant representation.

Church World Services (CWS), the National Council of Churches (NCC), NSCC, and SCC work together to help those in need in north and south Sudan, although the most critical needs are in the south. Help is provided regardless of race, religion, or political affiliation. Most of the Christians are in the south, and many of the people attend church.

Persecution has centered on the Aweil province of the Bahr al-Ghazal region in southern Sudan for decades, aimed at the people living there and the church. This is Abraham Nhial's home; this is where his heart yearns for the people to know God and His Son Jesus Christ. Roman Catholics were the first to venture into the area, but in the last decade, the Episcopal Church of the Sudan has brought the hope of the gospel. In the beginning, the Christians who ministered to these people were more zealous about their faith than equipped with biblical knowledge.

Currently, there are about fifty Episcopalian priests in the freed areas of Aweil. Of this number, only five are theologically trained and some are deacons. Eight of the priests are in northern Sudan. This small number shares the responsibilities of more than 150 congregations. The immediate needs in Aweil province are a concrete building to use as a training facility for the priests and to store supplies. The evangelists need to be equipped with Bible knowledge so that they can minister effectively. Funds are needed to purchase training materials and to transport them into the most devastated areas of southern Sudan. It is crucial for these new priests to be educated and encouraged in their faith so they can assist their people.

The SCC works primarily in the north to help those who are displaced, by educating women in health and nutrition, by helping people establish projects that will initiate income, and by encouraging unity among the people.

The NSCC was established in 1991 to serve southern Sudan in peace-making efforts and promote conferences to help tribes settle disputes. To date, problems among the tribes have been drastically reduced.

Christian organizations from outside Sudan also provide assistance to local believers and pastors.

For example, the Voice of the Martyrs has delivered more than 200,000 blankets, sixty thousand life packs, and thousands of Bibles to help the needy people of southern Sudan. The packs each contain a Bible, a blanket, mosquito netting, a bucket, water purification tablets, pots, pans, cups, plates, utensils, a rope, a hoe, soap, salt, thread, knives, needles, matches, razor blades, and a carrying bag. They may also contain a tarp and fabric to filter water. Ted Dodd says, "When we find pastors with no means to reach the people they seek to minister, we are often able to provide a bicycle."[1]

Approximately 23.14 percent or 6,836,666 people in Sudan are Christians. Because many Sudanese are fleeing persecution for their Christian faith, congregations have sprung up in areas that have never before heard the gospel. In 1960, the Christian population in Sudan was growing at a rate of 5 percent. By the year 2000, this figure was nearly 70 percent. For the last fifty years, the government has attempted to eliminate the church in Sudan, but the figures show it is failing. God will continue to draw people to Him despite the intense persecution.

Santino Bol Akook, a Sudanese Episcopal minister, recounts his experiences with Islamic persecution, his conversion to Christianity, and ministry in Sudan.

"I was born in Awiel West County in Awiel District in southern Sudan to a family that hardly knew about the gospel; neither did all the surrounding people know about this gospel. My parents believed in their forefathers' gods, which they relied on to solve all of the problems in the society.

"I belonged to a clan known as Paciny that had a magician called Dengdit, meaning 'great evil.' Dengdit was adored very much and feared by our clan as well as the other clans of the Sudanese Dinka community. All of these clans were also expected to offer sacrifices of cereals and other foodstuffs. In our clan, it was a requirement that each parent was supposed to offer a heifer cow upon the marriage of every firstborn daughter and so did my parents when my older sister got married. It was believed the daughter would not bear children until fulfillment of the ritual.

"Before my mother came to know the Lord, she was an agent of Dengdit. She was always called upon to organize other women to sing praise songs in adoration to Dengdit and to petition in case of such problems as droughts, sickness, and other disasters. In our compound, we had a Dengdit granary where the entire offering was kept until it was sizable enough and my mother mobilized the women to deliver it to Dengdit.

"In 1983, the current civil war broke out as a result of oppression by the Islamic government. At this time President Jaafaral al-Nimeiri was in power. After this came another president, Sadiq al-Mahdi, who was worse. He decided to mobilize vigilante groups known as Arab cattle raiders. These *mujahadeen* took all the livestock from the black Sudanese community. At the time I was in the cattle camp tending our cattle. With my life in danger, I decided to go to exile in Ethiopia, a neighboring country. What was in my mind was to acquire a gun from Ethiopia to get revenge on the Arabs for having robbed and killed my relatives and friends.

"While in Ethiopia living in the refugee camp, I heard God's voice and I accepted Christ as my personal Savior in 1986. I then started my primary education until completed. I also served in church as a Sunday school teacher. After this, my pastor saw I had a talent for evangelism and put me in ministry. I continued my secondary schooling, but when I was almost through, a different regime came to power in Ethiopia. This happened in early 1990, and the regime did not want the Sudanese refugees. We had to run away. A great flood drowned many people. We lost almost everything including certificates and other things we had.

"Upon expulsion (from the Ethiopian refugee camp), I came to a refugee camp in Kenya. I immediately decided to go back to Sudan as I had a call to evangelize my people back home. I then started ministry work, and God has seen me this far. I now have a congregation of 17,500 members. I thank God for that. These members are distributed among the fifty Protestant congregations in northern Bahr al-Ghazal.

"I still experience a lot of slavery raids and burning of churches as well as killing of the Christian believers. Within the area of evangelism, I thank God that the more the church is oppressed, the more the church grows stronger. However, I have a burden to pray to God in order to let peace come. CSI came in 1995, and I have been working with them as a senior pastor as well as the founder of the Episcopalian Church in this area. I have twelve pastors assisting me in the fifty congregations. I make sure I visit my wife and family in Kenya often. Thank you, and God bless you all."

I raise my eyes toward the mountains.
Where will my help come from?
My help comes from the LORD,
the Maker of heaven and earth.

PSALM 121:1–2

Chapter Twelve

America the Springboard

Abraham's journey to the United States in 2001 held new and strange encounters. He recalls that the three-day orientation before boarding the plane did not fully prepare him or the other boys for the changes awaiting them.

The Lost Boys' transition to life in the United States involved training that could be achieved only by living with American traditions and culture. No amount of orientation, reading material, or advice beforehand could prepare them for day-to-day activities in the United States. After arriving here, they had to adjust quickly to a new, fast-paced, stressful lifestyle: bumper-to-bumper traffic, rapid transportation, cell phones, fast food, American vocabulary and slang, billboards and advertisements for items they've never heard of or thought they needed, and overwhelming choices in grocery stores, restaurants, and malls. To some of them, this sudden change was as frightening as their lives in Sudan.

The young men speak and read English, but often their accents made communication difficult. Where once there was a sea of ebony faces, there's now a mixture of Caucasian, Latino, Asian, and a whole range of brown to black skin. Apartment living is a challenge to the senses: the sound of a flushing toilet or the hum of a refrigerator, the sight of gadgets in a modern kitchen, the tastes and smells of unusual foods, the touch of a solid wall instead of a tent or rough shelter, and the softness of carpet underfoot.

"We were excited and a little scared too," Abraham says. "The plane ride was not my first. The journey to America was tiring, but I was excited. For many of the Lost Boys, this first plane frightened them. They thought they were going to fall down. We had been through so many dangers, and this looked like one more. At every airport—in Europe and in New York—we were met by INS staff people who assisted us in getting on the right flight. These were caring people who wondered how we were doing. We were shocked at the new way of dressing. I arrived in New York in May 2001. Immediately I was welcomed by staff members from the *60 Minutes* TV program. I flew on to Atlanta where I met representatives from the Christian Council of Metropolitan Atlanta (CCMA) and again staff members from *60 Minutes*."

The boys were not treated as foreigners but as sons and brothers home from a long trip. To Abraham, this was a sign from God that they were in a good place. Refugee Resettlement and Immigration Services of Atlanta (RRISA) met Abraham and some of the other brothers at the airport and escorted them to Jubilee Partners, a Christian organization that helps refugees. Staff and volunteers taught Abraham and the other boys how to cook, use appliances, clean, and wash clothes. They assisted the brothers in employment opportunities, education options, and counseling in meeting emotional as well as physical needs.

The experience for Abraham was like a dream. "My head seemed to be swimming with all that was happening." Despite his apprehension about coming to America, he felt blessed to be met by many friendly, helpful people.

"My first job was to help other Lost Boys establish goals, become aware of the new surroundings, and obtain funds for school and other needs. My second job was working with my church, the Sudanese Episcopal Church of Atlanta. This is what I really like to do. I love the work and the people."

School came next. "First, I attended pre-GED [general equivalency diploma] classes, and now I'm enrolled at Atlanta Christian College. My degree will be a bachelor of science in biblical studies, and I have about two and a half years until I graduate. I also attended the College of Biblical Studies in Houston for a couple of fast-track courses. I want to become a minister and someday return to Sudan and lead my people in faith for Jesus Christ."

Although many of the Lost Boys attended school in the refugee camps, they still need to pursue a GED in the United States. The student must obtain a test score of at least 60 percent to pursue higher education. This involves a knowledge of language arts, including reading, and social studies, science, and mathematics. In addition, the applicant must complete an essay on a topic given at the time of the testing. Across the country, volunteers are assisting the Lost Boys to obtain these diplomas so they can pursue a college education.

These men have aspirations to become lawyers, pastors, teachers, accountants, engineers, law enforcement officers, social workers, medical personnel, political leaders, and agricultural specialists.

Each Lost Boy must have a job. They have come to the United States with little or no money. They depend on public transportation, bicycles, or walking to get them where they need to go.

Apartment buildings have strict rules and guidelines for new tenants. They require security deposits along with utility deposits. How can refugees obtain housing without money or employment? How will the Lost Boys furnish their new homes? Who teaches them how to cook, clean, pay bills, establish a budget? Who mentors them when they need advice?

If the Lost Boys are not carefully guided, they can fall prey to undesirable relationships that threaten them as seriously as the soldiers and perilous conditions that drove them from their homes. Without a good support system, instead of achieving his goals, a Lost Boy, sadly, may find despair and loneliness that could lead to crime or substance abuse. But that's where volunteers enter the picture.

Volunteers and Sponsors

Volunteers are needed in every aspect of the refugees' lives in the United States. Perhaps you are one who would like to help, but you don't know how to get started. Use the following three guidelines to determine if this is God's plan for you.

1. Pray. The world is full of worthwhile projects in which Christians can be involved. But only God knows if you are to make a difference in a Lost Boy's life. Ask God to

lead you to the proper organization involved with this type of project.

2. Contact churches and humanitarian organizations in your community to see if a program for the Lost Boys has been established. Whether you're led to be a part of a team of volunteers or to begin a core group yourself, these people are more than willing to share their knowledge.

3. Search the Internet for organizations that represent the Lost Boys. They offer expertise and put potential volunteers in contact with the Sudanese.

Certain steps will assure sponsors of success with the fewest headaches and problems. Frank Blackwood, director of Aid Sudan Foundation, has approximately 160 Lost Boys in his care. When approached by people who desire to sponsor these young men, Frank spends hours screening them. In essence, he is building a level of trust. The Lost Boys are *his* children. He wants to make sure the potential sponsor's heart is in tune with God before continuing the "adoption process." Frank and his associates coach the sponsors in preparation for many situations. A commitment to these young men is not a decision to be made lightly.

William and Julia Gray of Houston tried to ignore God's prompting to help the Lost Boys, but everywhere they turned, someone or something prompted a reminder of the need. When Julia saw one of the Lost Boys riding a bicycle, she decided it was time to help. God had gotten her attention.

First, Blackwood showed the *60 Minutes* video about the Lost Boys (from May 2002) to the Gray's church's mission board. (Since then, another *60 Minutes* program about the Lost Boys aired in January 2003.) Once the board members were behind the project for their church, the Grays invited these church leaders to their home for dinner, when a member of the Aid Sudan Foundation discussed the process of placing four Lost Boys in the area.

An announcement appeared in their church bulletin about the need for jobs, housing, furnishings, leadership roles, and mentors. The women's ministry showed the *60 Minutes* film, then organized a church-wide "shower" through which church members provided items the boys needed. The Lost Boys received everything they needed plus enough money to pay the security deposit on an apartment, the utilities, rent, and food.

The process of finding jobs for the Lost Boys came as a miracle. Julia approached a hospital in her area for job applications. She visited with the head of the human resources department who indicated an immediate need for food service help. The hospital had decided to end a contract with a catering service and take on the responsibility of food preparation and service in-house. To the department director, these young men were an answer to a problem. To the Grays, the potential job placement was an answer to prayer. The director waived the normal application process and had the Lost Boys' information e-mailed directly to her.

Usually, finding an apartment can be time-consuming and costly, and rules are stringent. The Grays found a beautiful two-bedroom apartment for which the leasing agent bent the rules to allow the four Lost Boys to live in the same apartment; the apartment's rules had stated a maximum of three unrelated persons could live together. In addition, the leasing agent omitted the usual background check and reduced the amount of rent. The agent did not know the reduced rent equaled the exact amount budgeted by the Lost Boys.

Volunteers helped the Lost Boys move into their new home with new and used furnishings, along with bicycles for transportation. The day became a gala celebration. A committee showed the boys how to cook, clean, and shop. Another volunteer escorted them to a local college and assisted them in enrolling.

A number of the volunteer organizations have adopted bylaws to establish communication between the Lost Boys and the volunteers. These guidelines incorporate spiritual, educational, cultural, and social goals in an effort to establish self-sufficient Christian leaders for a global community. The bylaws clearly outline the role of the volunteer and the mission outlook for the organization sponsoring the Lost Boys.

Under spiritual development, the Lost Boys commit to place God first, become involved with a local church, and to participate in Bible study classes. The sponsors pledge to assist the young men by helping them grow closer to God, discover His purpose for their lives, and develop godly friendships.

Education is vital. Each Lost Boy commits to making education a high priority, utilizing his gifts and talents, studying hard in his classes, and to assuming personal responsibility for future growth. The volunteers pledge to support the young men in every way possible. They arrange fund-raisers for education. Committees determine how the money is used.

Financial responsibility can be a burden for the Lost Boys and the sponsors. Clear guidelines outline expectations. For most cases, the young men are placed in an apartment in groups of two to four. They are responsible for equal portions of rent, utilities, and food. They are also expected to equally share the housework, cooking, and the overall upkeep of the apartment. Money sent back to Sudan to help families, tribes, clans, and villages is to be minimal. The best way these young men can help their country is to pursue an education.

Abraham paid back the initial funds he received from INS when he entered the United States. He lives with a strict budget of $850 per month. With these funds, he sends money to his wife and to his sister Rebecca in Kenya, pays rent, car insurance, gas, food, and any incidentals. There is no money for illness or unexpected expenses. He has not had to see a doctor since living in the United States. God is his provider, and Abraham knows He will take care of him.

"I learned how to care for a bicycle in Kakuma," Abraham says. "That helped me when I got to the United States and received my own. I have my driver's license and I do have a car, but I take MARTA to school—Atlanta's public transportation."

Sponsors often provide bicycles along with safety equipment and instructions on proper maintenance. Workshops educate the young men on how to change a tire, measure air pressure, adjust the brakes, elevate the seat, and grease and degrease the chain. Owning and financially maintaining a vehicle can be costly and time-consuming and is discouraged.

Volunteers have learned that occasionally a Lost Boy needs additional mentoring and requires professional counseling. Some of them resent rules, guidelines, and directives, even if the instructions are in their best interests. Who taught the Lost Boys values? Who provided them with physical, emotional, intellectual, and spiritual guidance? Who showed them a level of maturity when they were one another's parents? The answer to these questions is simple: their peers. Are they to be treated as boys or men? Obviously, these Sudanese are men, and treating them as boys is not only condescending but does not develop a level of trust between them and the mentors.

Sponsors and volunteers must prayerfully consider their roles in the mentoring process. All aspects take time, patience, and wise counsel from those who have previously worked with the Lost Boys and professional counselors. Ongoing training sessions and group meetings to discuss problem areas, support other mentors, and share success stories with the Lost Boys are vital. Planning and organization helps eliminate frustrations on the part of the mentors and the Lost Boys.

These young men are not accustomed to trust; it must be earned. The Lost Boys may share a common tragedy, but they have been created with strengths and weaknesses. The positive is to be encouraged and nurtured; the negative must be guided along a different path. The Lost Boys' uniqueness is a gift from God intended for His purpose. Proper communication is the key to a successful relationship between the Sudanese and those who desire to lend a helping hand. Prayer is the doorway to understanding.

Victor Deng Akec Majok, a Lost Boy, thanks those who have helped him: "I was born in Wau, Sudan, and lived in the village of Pannyok. I am the sixth of eight children. My father was killed when I was young because of his belief in Jesus. He taught me about Jesus. I became a Christian when I was four years old, and now I want to become a preacher and tell others about Jesus. So that I can learn more about the Bible and Jesus, I attend a Bible study near where I live.

"I work at a church as a custodian. I like my job and I like going to school. I am taking a prealgebra class at the college.

"I want to thank all of the people who have helped us. They have helped us get into college and find us a nice place to live. They have given us furniture and computers to do our homework and to learn on. They have tutored us and helped us learn to shop and to do cooking, although most of us are still not doing so well with cooking.

"Please pray for me and my education and my journey in becoming a preacher. Proverbs 3:5–6 says: 'Trust in the Lord with all your heart, and lean not on your own understanding; in all your ways acknowledge Him, and He shall direct your paths.'

"God bless you, and God bless America."

" 'For I know the plans I have for you,' says the Lord. 'They are plans for good and not for evil, to give you a future and a hope.' "

Jeremiah 29:11

Six Lost Boys who are on their way to becoming successful. They live in the Woodlands, Texas, and have a strong support group through churches and community. (Photograph used with permission.)

Abraham is thankful for the support of others too. Jamie and Jodi Herring, a volunteer couple from North Carolina, helped Abraham extensively to assist the Lost Boys. This particular couple flew to Atlanta and brought other Lost Boys to visit Abraham. Jodi has arranged several speaking engagements for Abraham. They have partnered with Abraham for improvement projects in Kakuma, especially with the Zone Six Episcopal Church, which Abraham served as a pastor. Jodi introduced Abraham to Brad Phillips, president of Persecution Project Foundation, who is a strong advocate for the cause of the southern Sudanese. In his video, "Oil Fueled Genocide," Phillips speaks out against the atrocities committed in southern Sudan. He is a personal friend of Abraham.

In addition, the Reverend Tom Stubbs of the Episcopal Diocese of Atlanta has mentored Abraham, advising him in various matters of his new life.

To Abraham, volunteers across the United States who assist the Lost Boys are lifelines. "They ensure that the Lost Boys are safe, attend school, obtain medical treatment, dental treatment, secure jobs, and act as family. We love you and thank you for all of your hard work."

Health Issues

According to Abraham, "Poor nutrition is a big part of the Lost Boys' health problems. Many don't know they are sick. They've felt the pain for so long that they don't recognize it as abnormal. They need special attention, good doctors, and checkups."

Reuben Luai Thic was born in 1977 in southern Sudan. GOS forces attacked his village when he was eight years old. He

walked into an Ethiopian refugee camp in 1987, where he stayed
for six years. "In 1991, the Ethiopians ran us out of the camps to
force us back into southern Sudan," Reuben says. "Ethiopia was
having their troubles at the time, so the Ethiopian government
told us to leave. I went to Nasr in southern Sudan. In Nasr the
GOS attacked us. Soldiers shot me in the upper left thigh. I spent
three days in the bush."

Reuben spent three years in Khartoum, one year of that time
in prison. Eventually he was accepted by the U.S. refugee program and came to the United States in December 1999.

"Sometimes when I try to sleep, I ask God to give life back to
my leg. It has been very tough, but God promised that He had
plans for me to help the people of Sudan. So when I find good
people here who take me to the hospital and doctor appointments and show me love, then I know Americans love people.

"Since arriving in the United States, I have had five major
surgeries to repair my leg. My leg was in a metal brace for more
than two years, and now I have physical therapy five times a
week. I will continue to do this until I can bend my leg. The doctors say it will take years, but I am determined to work hard in
therapy so that my healing can be complete."

The Lost Boys experienced years of malnutrition before
entering Kakuma where they received only one bland meal a day.
Now that they are in the United States where food is plenty and
health care is easier to obtain, many of them, like Reuben, still
experience health concerns.

One common problem is the Lost Boys' aversion to drinking
tap water. Most of them choose sugar-sweetened beverages. The
young men report the taste of water reminds them too much of

the dirty water in Africa. They remember the sickness and disease from foul streams, and although the water in the United States is potable, the memory lingers. Caring Americans can reeducate the Lost Boys in the value of good drinking water and help them incorporate it in their daily diets.

The Lost Boys have undergone numerous vaccinations and a thorough physical to apply for their green cards—a U.S. document that allows aliens to live and work in the United States. In addition, they are tested for tuberculosis and HIV. The results are not given to them until they are approved as U.S. refugees. Some of the Lost Boys have had positive TB tests, although chest X-rays have cleared them to work.

A number have a high bilirubin count. Symptoms are yellow eyes, dark urine, and yellow skin. High bilirubin counts can indicate liver disease.

"Some of the brothers have been very sick and required surgery," Abraham says. "During those days when we walked, disease grew because of no doctors or medicine. Stomachache is the most common complaint from us. I think this is due to our past poor nutrition and eating things that aren't for human consumption. We ate leaves and tree bark to survive, and countless other things that only animals eat. Another problem is headaches. We were forced across deserts, and Kakuma is a hot, desolate place. I am fortunate to be in good health now."

Along with the headaches is low blood sugar, often because the Lost Boys don't make eating a priority. It's easy for them to ignore hunger or thirst signals because of their one-meal-a-day schedule in the refugee camp. Sponsors and friends report that it is not unusual for them to skip eating for a few days in order to send money to Africa. This is highly discouraged. Volunteers and mentors teach them that they cannot help their people if they do not take care of themselves.

"Stomach parasites are also a common disorder," Abraham continues. "In Africa we had a problem with typhoid too. For those who have had serious illnesses and recovered, permanent damage has been done to their bodies.

"Back in Kakuma, I got sick with malaria and was admitted to the hospital for a week. That was the first time that I had ever been that sick or in a hospital. I'm too busy all the time to be sick. I pray God will protect me and not allow all the things I do to wipe me out. I don't get enough rest. I'm in a different climate, with different people. We are eating chemicals and preservatives here, and that is new to our bodies. We also eat more sugar and fat. In Kakuma, we had only one meal a day, but it gave us energy to keep going. I wonder if the variety of foods in the United States confuses our bodies."

The Lost Boys take pride in personal cleanliness, and their dwellings are immaculate. They do get tired physically because they often ride bicycles or walk for transportation. They also have the demands of jobs, school, homework, and extracurricular activities. Sponsors and enthusiastic volunteers often fail to see the stress they place on the Sudanese refugees, especially when they want their community and friends to become acquainted with these courageous young men. Sponsors need to be reminded that their role is to guide and mentor the Lost Boys and not to place them on display or direct every minute of their day.

Many of the Lost Boys believed seeing a doctor meant going to the emergency room. Sponsors have educated them in the process of making an appointment with a doctor who has an office and to be prepared for the paperwork. One young man reported he'd rather be sick than complete the overwhelming number of medical forms.

Because many of the Lost Boys use bicycles for transportation, accidents are common. Most of them feel their lives are in danger from careless drivers. Too many of them have been hit by vehicles, and one Lost Boy died after being hit by a car.

Another fear is dogs because of the refugees' experiences with wild dogs in Africa. One young man exhibited tremendous fear when a volunteer asked if he would like to accompany him on a nightly walk with his dog. Not only was the young man afraid of the dog; he also feared an attack by lions. Communication between the Lost Boys and sponsors can eliminate this type of stress.

Proper dental care is another concern. Fortunately, most of the Lost Boys have excellent teeth. Because they haven't eaten a lot of processed sugar, they have solid bones, few cavities, and healthy gums. In Kakuma, most of the boys used a bundle of sticks to brush their teeth. The problem now is that some of the Lost Boys had their six bottom teeth removed through a tribal ritual in Sudan. When the boys are between the ages of seven and nine, an instrument similar to a screwdriver is used to "flick" out the teeth. The boys are instructed not to cry, for in doing so they are shunned and lose the opportunity to secure a wife in later years. Bravery and manhood are exhibited by not showing pain. It often takes months before the ache subsides in the boy's mouth. The side effects of this procedure are the inability to eat some foods and to pronounce words correctly. Abraham had his teeth extracted, too, but a volunteer dentist in Atlanta restored his smile.

The Lost Boys report that the practice of extracting the lower teeth has been abandoned in their generation. The ritual is now a choice for the young boy. The more educated the village, the less likely for the practice to continue.

Missing teeth have also occurred from accidents, conflicts while in Africa, and tribal fighting. One young man lost two teeth when a cow became out of control. The Lost Boys who experienced ritual extraction of teeth now desire a healthy, pleasing smile. This is a costly procedure and for many a hope for the future. They understand their appearances do not reflect Western culture and become a source of humiliation for them.

Medical professionals from all over the country have offered their time and services to help the Lost Boys.

In some communities, sponsors and volunteers act as medical advisers. They help the Lost Boys manage their health care by accompanying them to doctor and dental appointments, advocating for them, interpreting doctor or dentist instructions, and teaching them how to take prescriptions.

Mental Health

Other concerns plague the Lost Boys. Abraham says, "We share in many of the same personal goals. We want Sudanese wives not American wives, and we need money to bring the women here and the proper government forms to make this possible. The money is simply not available. It is difficult for the Lost Boys to do much more than pay their share of food, rent, and utilities—and educational expenses. The dilemma affects the boys mentally, causing more depression. They need help and understanding. Without wives, too many Lost Boys cannot concentrate on work and school goals. If they marry American girls and stay here, they will lose their culture and not return to their country. The Sudanese people will be lost, and who will lead Sudan when it is free? The girls will not wait for boyfriends and husbands for five to six years. This is a real problem."

Although the Lost Boys received assistance and opportunities when they entered the United States, they are not immune to depression in a land not their own. From the wilds of Africa to American shores is a culture shock. Sometimes the United States is too big, too loud, too busy, and too fast for a young man accustomed to a slower pace of life.

Many of the Lost Boys struggle with anxiety. In order to combat this despair, they tend to stay active. They often worry about their loved ones in Africa and are torn over how to help them and how to take care of themselves. It's difficult for them to know where to draw the line between these two needs. The hardships in Sudan are vivid, and none of the Lost Boys want their loved ones to suffer, so they sometimes forgo their own necessities in order to send money back to loved ones in Kenya or Sudan.

Humanitarian groups, churches, and volunteers can help the refugees with physical needs, but loneliness can be harder to fight than a visible enemy.

One Lost Boy relates, "To begin with, I'd like to talk about my life experience when I first came to the States. Life was full of depression and culture shock, and unless you have ever been in a new country with separation from your family, you cannot know how I feel. Have you ever experienced that? I am in much depression now in the USA, and even last year I was told by the doctor that I shouldn't be thinking very much like that, otherwise it will be very harmful to my life here. There is no way I can avoid that because I just want to recall the times when I was with my family. This is why my depression keeps increasing, and to me it is very uncontrollable. I can't give up thinking about my daughter and my lovely wife. We were married in February 2001, the same year I came to the United States. It is very impossible, but for now I put all my possibilities in God the Father's hand. If He is the Almighty Father of all the earth, He will definitely solve my problem, and I trust in Him.

"However, America is a wonderful place where we can raise our families and work and live. I think my goals are to unite with my family and get good education, and then I can give my support to my country through money or education. I can do one of the two."

This young man is walking through sadness. In one breath, his faith in God sustains him. In the next breath, the overwhelming unhappiness threatens to consume him. He and others like him need mentors to guide and direct them in their new lives. Some of the Lost Boys refer to these volunteers as parents, aunts, or uncles. Their childhood was lost, and their families were destroyed—and they crave meaningful relationships.

One young man found an outlet for his suffering. Atem Thuc Aleu lives and works in Salt Lake City. He is the only surviving member of his family. In Kakuma he studied art as well as other subjects. When he came to the United States in March 2001, he brought his oil paintings illustrating refugee life and the effects of war on the Sudanese. These originals were painted on mosquito netting, not canvas. A showing of his work and a reception to honor the Sudanese community was hosted by the Art Access II Gallery in Salt Lake City.

"Things in the school were hard because I had to struggle with how to survive. It was hard for me to go to the best school due to many problems because nobody could pay for my school. In 1994, the thought came to me that I could be an artist in order to solve [deal with] my problems and remember what happened to my family and my country. I started to paint by using water-color, then through acrylic and oil. Most of my paintings are from memory, observation, and imagination, so I can draw and paint about what happened in my daily life to help people under-stand what happened to me. While in Kakuma, I got my art sup-plies from the Episcopal Church and UNHCR."

His involvement in the art program and gallery in Utah has helped him show his paintings. "I thank all the people of the United States, especially the government for their help and mercy on poor people like me, who haven't seen their families for four-teen years. I ask God to bless the USA and my homeland, espe-cially those who struggle for southern Sudan."

Atem Thuch Aleu painting entitled Sudanese Refugees.
(Courtesy of Borge B. Anderson & Associates and Arts Program
of the Utah Arts Council. Used with permission.)

Yahweh my Lord is my strength;
He makes my feet like those of a deer
and enables me to walk on mountain heights!

HABAKKUK 3:19

Chapter Thirteen

A Wedding and the Future

Abraham Nhial traveled to Kakuma in June 2003 to marry Daruka Aloung Bior. Daruka means "a deer." Before he left Kenya in 2001, Abraham realized his love for her and wanted to marry her one day. According to their culture, he first approached his relatives and told them he wanted Daruka for his wife. From that point, his relatives searched her family background and asked questions about her personality and mannerisms. Their appraisal was to determine if Daruka would be a good wife for Abraham.

Daruka also called her family together and revealed her love for Abraham. She told them of their desire to marry. In turn, her relatives did the same type of research about Abraham.

If either family decided that one of the two were unsuitable, the marriage would not occur. The man could be wealthy or hold a high position, but if he was not a good man and would not take care of the woman properly, the family would not permit the

161

marriage. The same for Daruka; Abraham's family must be convinced that she would love and honor him as a husband.

Once Abraham's and Daruka's families agreed to the match,
the relatives began negotiations for the dowry. In most instances,
the prospective groom's family assists in the dowry. For Daruka's
dowry, the bride's family received one hundred cows. Abraham
received financial help from relatives and friends in Africa and the
United States to help pay the bride-price. Because of the lack of
grass and water in Kakuma, the bride's father accepted money to
purchase cows when peace comes to Sudan, and they are able to
return to fertile land. Abraham's father did travel to Kenya for
Abraham and Daruka's wedding in June 2003, but he later
returned to southern Sudan.

At the ceremony, the nineteen-year-old bride wore a white
dress, and Abraham wore a dark suit, just like in a Western marriage ceremony. After two weeks of married life, Abraham
returned to Atlanta and began to work toward saving money and
submitting the INS forms for Daruka to enter the United States.
Once the papers are approved, Abraham will need to send her
money to purchase airfare. After the marriage, Daruka kept her
name. Her wedding ring and conservative dress now distinguish
her as a married woman.

"It is very hard for my wife to be in Kenya," Abraham says.
"I miss her and try to call her twice a week. She always cries. I
send money to her where she lives in Nakuru, Kenya. There she
is receiving her high school education. I want my wife to be an
educated lady. I also send money for my sister Rebecca."

As a married couple, Abraham and Daruka desire to further
their education and then help others. They plan to spread the

gospel as missionaries to southern Sudan. Someday they would like to have children.

Although the weeks and months ahead look difficult, Abraham and Daruka are filled with hope and wait expectantly for what God purposes through their lives.

Abraham says, "In June 2003 when I went back to the refugee camp in Kakuma, I was reminded about my experiences of survival in Africa. I understand how blessed I am to be living in this country and how many of my brothers and sisters still remain in Sudan with the constant fear of death. I have the opportunity to go to school, work, security, food, shelter, and many other things, but my people in Sudan lack these. None of us here can forget our mission."

As this book is written, Abraham has lived in the United States for two years and nine months. Currently, he works for Bridging the Gap, a nonprofit organization, in various projects since 2001. He helps raise funds for the Lost Boys' education and medical care. He also works with the All Saints Episcopal Church and the Episcopal Diocese of Atlanta, which has supported and encouraged him and his church, the Sudanese Episcopal Church of Atlanta.

Abraham, also a board member for the Aid Sudan Foundation, is assisting Frank Blackwood, director, in planning a mission trip back to villages of southern Sudan in 2005. Abraham is coordinating this project. The goal is to lead a select group of Lost Boys back to their old villages with the gospel of Jesus Christ.

Not all of the Lost Boys can deal with their wounds of the past. The pain evident in their eyes reveals the grief and sorrow for the loss of their family, friends, home, and country. For many, the thought of reliving the nightmares is inconceivable—best forgotten, even denied. Some out of fear chose not to have their names mentioned, and still others wanted the world to hear what is happening in their homeland.

Abraham is one who speaks for the oppressed people of southern Sudan. "The Lost Boys are a group of Sudanese young men who were separated from their parents and families in a horrible civil war. Too many have been killed. Our mission is to work for the future of southern Sudan. We need a new Sudan, new people, and a new government that will care for its citizens. We are here in the United States for education to become doctors, engineers, pastors, and teachers. We must have knowledge to build our country. We need American churches, the government, and individuals with goodwill to help us achieve our dreams and ambitions for Sudan, and for the whole world. We are true survivors and are willing to work hard and share our hearts. During the tragedy on September 11, 2001, we collected money for the Red Cross. We know what it's like to lose loved ones because we have lost those we love too."

Besides Abraham and Daruka's personal goals, Abraham also has dreams for Sudan's political and spiritual future. He begs for the world to initiate more peace-making efforts. "The Lost Boys dream of a new southern Sudan and a new Nuba Mountain region. The world needs to know there is a state of 'New Sudan,' and these people need to be given the right to govern themselves in freedom. We pray for a time when the people will work for their own benefit and for the benefit of generations to follow.

"As Christians, we still love the GOS, but they do not love us. They want to lead the people of Sudan. In Atlanta, the Sudanese brothers share the same apartment complex with our Muslim brothers, but they do not call us brothers. We eat together and talk together, but they do not think as Christian brothers.

"In June 2001, I went to Washington, D.C., with the Ethics and Religious Liberty Commission (ERLC). There I learned that Sudan is one of six countries that deny religious freedom. The others are Burma, China, Iran, Iraq, and North Korea. Since that time, the Iraqi people have been given their freedom by the United States. Just as we had Operation Iraqi Freedom, we need Operation Sudanese Freedom.

"While in Washington, I met Sadiq al-Mahdi, the prime minister of Sudan, who ordered the killing of my people when I left home in 1987. I told him I loved him, but we need peace in Sudan."

Al-Mahdi was surprised at Abraham's words. "Why do they call you a Lost Boy? They need to call you Peace Boy," al-Mahdi told him.

Abraham responded, "Whether you call me Lost Boy or Peace Boy is not your or my concern. The real concern is peace in Sudan. The southern Sudanese are so ready for peace, but the GOS is not ready."

Abraham believes that throughout the cease-fire and peace talk, the GOS hides its agenda. "We've had enough talk and no action, and we southerners should be given our own country. I believe we can rule ourselves. We've been fighting for twenty years, and it shows me that we can govern ourselves effectively.

"It has been proven through church and humanitarian organizations that the GOS is involved in genocide. They support worldwide terrorists. What happened on September 11, 2001, in the United States was not new to the Sudanese people. We'd seen this type of activity for years."

Abraham takes a deep breath. "When I speak about this situation with my people, I do not want to convince Americans that they are to go there and kill the Muslims, but we do need freedom to worship.

"Americans should know we are sharing the world with a complicated people. In my heart, I believe we need to share the love of Christ with the Muslims but not force them, as an act of love. We need to be very careful with our Muslim brothers here in the United States. When I arrived here and saw how fast the Muslim religion is growing in the Western world, it alarmed me. In the very beginning when the Muslims came to Sudan, they were very good people, but as they increased, they pushed the Christians out. The ideal of the Muslim is this. The ones who caused 9/11 came from among those living in the United States. They infiltrate from within.

"So how do we show the Muslims how to value human life? The truth is they can't because they don't have Jesus. So what do we do? The international community needs to take this seriously.

"More than four million people have died. The government has not changed its policies. Their mission is to convert all of Africa to Islam. What we need from the Western world is to say enough is enough and bring peace to Sudan. How many people must die before the Western world takes action? How many generations of black Africans are to be sacrificed in this war?"

Practical Needs

The leaders of southern Sudan understand that they must fight the GOS and build the country at the same time. Roads and bridges must be constructed. Currently, humanitarian organizations are forced to air-drop food and provisions because the GOS has forbidden them access or roads and bridges are in such deplorable condition that vehicles cannot transport the goods. The money required to transport these much-needed supplies could be used to purchase additional supplies.

To develop southern Sudan, good schools are essential for future growth and prosperity. Vocational training will equip the south to help people earn a living. Many desire to return to their old way of life—agricultural communities like they had for hundreds of years. Other southern Sudanese argue that the south needs to update its economy. A stable banking system is imperative to the success of a new nation. This will require communities to become involved in social and economic conditions.

Hospitals and clinics must be built to meet the ongoing health care needs and to combat disease in often epidemic proportions. Trained personnel are needed to assist men, women, and children in dealing with the psychological affects of the civil war.

"We want our country to grow and prosper. We want it to be self-reliant," Abraham says. "The education we receive in the United States prepares us for rebuilding our country."

Another Lost Boy expresses his views about his country: "My hope is to have a southern Sudan free from neocolonialism from Arabs and fundamentalists; a free south based on the ideals of mutual respect, tolerance, and recognition of culture and religious diversity. I also hope that southern Sudanese who have left Sudan because of war will return to their homeland. We need to rebuild the south; this is the reason we are fighting. Those who are fighting deserve to live in peace and prosperity once the war is over. The SPLA have spent their entire lives defending us, and they haven't had chances to get educated. They [southern Sudan] need us; they need our skills and knowledge."

Abraham dreams of bringing all of Sudan to a saving grace in Jesus Christ. He wants to raise his family free to worship and enjoy the benefits of a democracy. He wants to do all he can for the spiritual and economic development of Sudan.

"I do not want to go to God with empty hands. I am worried about the needs of so many people. I love them so much. I am praying and thinking about them all the time. I don't know exactly how I can take care of all their needs. Now, I know the difference between the camps and the United States. The Bible says there is a time for everything. I know there will be a time for them to be happy and feel at home."

We are pressured in every way but not crushed; we are perplexed but not in despair; we are persecuted but not abandoned; we are struck down but not destroyed.

2 CORINTHIANS 4:8–9

Acknowledgments

This book would not be possible without the encouragement and prayers of many people around the world. The following people have contributed so much, and many more need to be recognized: Frank Blackwood, director of Aid Sudan Foundation, this was your dream. Debbie Blackwood, for your prayers. Katie Brown, a representative of all who have given countless hours for the welfare of the Lost Boys. Gary Terashita, for believing in the project. Eric Reeves, who always answered questions. Dan Patrick, for his foreword to this book. Dean Mills, who wouldn't let me quit, Julia Duany of South Sudanese Friends International, Brad Phillips of Persecution Project Foundation, and Bobby Waddell of the Lutheran World Foundation.

Thank you for sharing your viewpoints, encouragement, life experiences, and prayers. The following people also helped form this book: Santino Akook, Atem Thuch Aleu, Abraham Akech, Kerby Anderson, Peter Athiang, Samson Jinga Augustin, Tony Barrett, Gail Bielitz, Sasha Chanoff, Caroline Cox, Abraham Deng, Petro Deng, William Deng, William Deng of Houston, Beau Egert, John Eibner, William and Julia Gray, Lisa Harris,

Jill Lindsey, Mark Littleton, Peter Malou, Sano Masua, Petro Maduk, Justin Pankow, Isobel Perry, Michael Rout, Laura Seay, Daniel Silvey, James Solomon, Reuben Luai Thic, Danny Uhyrek, Angelo Wol, and Santino Wol.

Abraham thanks: His church, the Sudanese Episcopal Church of Atlanta, for its cooperation and support. The Right Reverend Neil Alexander, for accepting him into the diocese as one of the clergy and for the love, support, and commitment. All Saints Episcopal Church, for its love and financial support. Tom Crick from the Carter Center in Atlanta. My two best friends: Clement Garang from Michigan. I helped him when he was younger, and now he gives me good advice. We are like brothers. And Richard Parkins, director of Episcopal Migration Ministry, for his commitment to pay for my high school in Kenya. He helped build my church in Kenya, changed my U.S. flight from Chicago to Atlanta, and is currently working to help my wife join me in America. Dr. Gail in Atlanta, for taking care of my lower teeth and for replacing the lower teeth for many Lost Boys. I am grateful to the Lost Boys' volunteers in Atlanta for their incredible work. I love you all! My three roommates and all of the Lost Boys in America, for their advice and encouragement during the writing of this book. Many thanks to Jamie and Jodi Herring for all they have done to help me and other Lost Boys. I especially want to thank Daruka, my dear wife. Sometimes I have forgotten to call her in Kenya due to school work and my work with the church, the Lost Boys, and this book. I love you for your understanding.

May God bless,

Abraham Nhial and DiAnn Mills

Notes

Chapter Four

1. "Sudan: Bush Signs Peace Act," UN Office for the Coordination of Humanitarian Affairs, *Irin News,* 30 October 2002, http://www.irinnews.org/report.asp?ReportID=30540& SelectRegion=East_Africa&SelectCountry=SUDAN (accessed 30 October 2002).

2. Julia Aker Duany, "Living between Despair and Hope: The Grassroots People of South Sudan," *South Sudan Friends,* 30 December 2002, http://www.southsudanfriends.org/Despair andhope.html.

Chapter Seven

1. Ergun Caner and Emir Caner, *Unveiling Islam* (Grand Rapids: Kregel, 2002), 241–51.

2. Kerby Anderson, Probe Ministries, information through e-mail conversation.

Chapter Eight

1. "The Scorched Earth: Oil and War in Sudan," *Christian Aid,* March 2001, http://www.christian-aid.org.uk/indepth/0103 suda/sudanoi2.htm#CHAP1 (accessed 9 April 2004).

2. Eric Reeves, "Rapacious Instincts in Sudan," *The Nation,* 4 June 2001.

3. Gerhart Baum, United Nations Human Rights investigator, *Civil War Becoming War over Oil—UN Report,* 10 October 2001.

4. Eric Reeves, "A UN Seat for Genocide," *The Washington Post,* 15 August 2001.

5. "SUDAN: Focus on oil-related clashes in western Upper Nile," IRINnews.org, February 2002, http://www.irinnews.org/report.asp?ReportID=23300&SelectRegion=EastAfrica&SelectCountry=SUDAN (accessed October 16, 2002).

6. "Canadian Oil Company Ordered Ethnic Cleansing in Sudan," *Abolish, the Anti-Slavery Portal,* March 2002, http://www.iabolish.com/news/global/2002/talisman03-05-02.htm (accessed October 16, 2002).

7. AFP—*Associated France Press,* Washington, 26 March 2003.

8. *The New York Times,* 31 March 2004.

Chapter Nine

1. "African Slavery Still," Tikkun.org, July/August 1999, http://www.tikkun.org/magazine/index.cfm/action/tikkun/issue/tik9907/article990713a.html (accessed June 2004); Ushari Ahmad Mahmud and Suleyman Ali Baldo, "Human Rights Violations in the Sudan," http://www.anti-slavery.org/pages/reports/diein.html (1987); Holland Webb, "Slavery in the Sudan," *Neo Politique,* http://www.neopolitique.org/Np2000/Pages/Essays/Articles/Sudan-slave%20redemption.htm (accessed June 2004).

2. Lucian Niemeyer, "The Sudan Slave Story," *Christian Solidarity International,* December 2000, http://www.lnsart.com/Sudan%20Slave%20Story.htm (accessed October 31, 2002).

3. Ibid.

4. Julia Aker Duany, "Living between Despair and Hope: The Grassroots People of South Sudan," *South Sudan Friends,* 30 December 2002, http://www.southsudanfriends.org/Despair andhope.html.

Chapter Ten

1. Frank Blackwood, director, Aid Sudan Foundation (Houston, Texas); interview.

2. Evans Mburu (director, IRC Adult Education), "Life in Kakuma, Kenya," *Enabling Education Network,* 5 October 2002, http://www.eenct.org.uk/newsletters/news6/page11.html (accessed October 31, 2002).

3. Jason Phillips (director, IRC Country), "Food Supplies Dwindle at Kakuma Refugee Camp, IRC Raises Concern in Washington," 4 June 2002, http://www.theirc.org/news/index/cfm?fa=newsdetail&newsID=905 (accessed October 31, 2002).

Chapter Eleven

1. Ted Dodd, Voice of the Martyrs, information through e-mail conversation.

Bibliography

Chapter One—Who Are Abraham Nhial and the Lost Boys of Sudan?

Levy, Patricia. *Sudan.* New York: Marshall Cavendish, 1951.

Page, Candace. "Lost Boys of Sudan: The Newest Vermonters." *Burlington Free Press,* 13 August 2001. http://www.burlington freepress.com/specialnews/sudan/ (accessed 8 April 2004).

Roddis, Ingrid. *Sudan.* Philadelphia: Chelsea House Publishers, 2000.

"Sudan," *Travel Document Systems,* 1996–2003. http://www.travel docs.com/sd/people.htm (accessed 8 April 2004).

"The Lost Boys of Sudan." *Servant's Heart,* 17 September 2001. http://www.sudanlostboys.com/disc1_frm.htm (accessed 8 April 2004).

U.S. Committee for Refugees. *World Refugee Survey 2001.* Washington, D.C.: U.S. Committee for Refugees, 108–15.

Chapter Two—Dinka Life and Culture

Archibald, Erika. *A Sudanese Family.* Minneapolis: Lerner Publications Company, 1997.

Buckley, Stephen. "Loss of Culturally Vital Cattle Leaves Dinka Tribe Adrift in Refugee Camps." *Washington Post Foreign Service,* 24 August 1997. http://www.washingtonpost.com/

wp-srv/inatl/longterm/africanlives/sudan/sudan.htm
(accessed 8 April 2004).

Ryle, John. *Warriors of the White Nile: The Dinka.* Amsterdam:
Time-Life Books, 1982.

"The Dinka of Sudan." *Sudan 101 People Groups.* http://www
.sudan101.com/dinka.htm (accessed 8 April 2004).

Chapter Three—The Endless Journey
Note references from chapter 1

Chapter Four—A Land Torn by Conflict

"About Sudan." Information Technology Associates, 1997.
http://www.theodora.com/wfb/sudan/sudan2.html (accessed
8 April 2004).

Duany, Julia Aker. "Living between Despair and Hope: The
Grassroots People of South Sudan." *South Sudan Friends,* 30
December 2002. http://www.southsudanfriends.org/Despair
andhope.html (accessed 8 April 2004).

Harmon, Donald E. *Sudan.* Philadelphia: Chelsea House
Publishers, 2001.

"Historical Setting." *Sudan, a Country Study.* http://www.lcweb2
.loc.gov/frd/cs/sdtoc.html (accessed 8 April 2004).

"History of Sudan." *Country Reports* 2002. http://www.country
reports.org/history/sudhist.htm (accessed 8 April 2004).

Holt, P. M. & M. W. Daly. *A History of the Sudan.* 5th ed. Essex,
England: Pearson Education Limited, 2000. "Sudan Flag
Description." *The World Factbook 2002.* http://www.cia.gov/cia/
publications/factbook/flags/su-flag.html (accessed 8 April 2004).

"Sudan, Republic of the Sudan." *Sudan: Facts on Sudan,* January

2001. http://www.sudan.net/fact.shtml (accessed 8 April 2004).

"The Flag, What It Stands For." *Sudan, Society, and Culture,* January 2001. http://www.sudan.net/society/flag.shtml (accessed 8 April 2004).

"Notice: Continuation of the National Emergency with Respect to Sudan." *Office of the Press Secretary,* 30 October 2002. http://www.whitehouse.gov/news/releases/2002/10/200210 30-3.html (accessed 9 April 2004).

Petterson, Donald. *Inside Sudan.* Boulder: Westview, 1999.

"Political Map of Sudan." Maps of Sudan, 2000. http://www.lib.utexas.edu/maps/africa/sudan_pol00.jpg (accessed 9 April 2004).

"President Asks Danforth to Continue to Serve as Envoy to Sudan." *Office of the Press Secretary,* 21 May 2002. http://www.whitehouse.gov/news/releases/2002/05/200205 21-6.html (accessed 9 April 2004).

"Secretariat on Peace in the Sudan." *Popular National Congress,* 20 July 2002, http://www.ncsudan.org/Machakos%20 Protocol%20.htm (accessed 9 April 2004).

"Sudan." *Bureau of Consular Affairs,* 6 August 2002. http://www.travel.state.gov/sudan.html (accessed 9 April 2004).

Chapter Five—Sudan People's Liberation Army

Barber, Mike. "Child Soldiers a Growing Concern on Foreign Battlefields." *Seattle Post Intelligencer-Reporter,* 8 April 2002. http://www.seattlepi.nwsource.com/national/65670_child soldiers08.shtml (accessed 9 April 2004).

"Jane's Sentinel Security Assessment, North Africa." *Jane's,* 26 June 2002. http://www.janes.com (accessed 9 April 2004).

Pelton, Robert. "History." *Sudan, the Country,* 2000. http://www .comebackalive.com/df/dplaces/sudan/ (accessed 9 April 2004).

"SPLA." *Sudan,* June 1991. http://www.reference.allrefer.com/ country-guide-study/sudan/sudan150.html (accessed 9 April 2004).

"The Sudanese People's Liberation Army." *A Country Study and a Country Guide,* June 1991. http://www.reference.allrefer.com/ country-guide-study/sudan/sudan150.html (accessed 9 April 2004).

"Sudan People's Liberation Movement/Army." *Intelligence Resource Program,* 5 January 2000. http://www.fas.org/irp/ world/para/spla.htm (accessed 9 April 2004).

"Sudan People's Liberation Movement/Army." *Welcome to the New Sudan official Site,* 20 March 2002. http://www.new sudanweb.com/ (accessed 9 April 2004).

Chapter Six—Life in Kakuma

Note References from chapter 1

Chapter Seven—Islam versus Christianity

Caner, Ergun and Emir Caner. *Unveiling Islam.* Grand Rapids: Kregel, 2002.

"English Translation of Al-Qur'an." Muslim Student Association of UMR, 1995. http://www.web.umr.edu/ ~msaumr/topics/index.html (accessed 8 April 2004).

Geisler, Norman L. and Abdul Saleeb. *Answering Islam.* Grand Rapids: Baker 2001.

McKenzie, Michael. "Onward Christian Soldiers?" *Christian Research Journal,* Fall 1996. http://www.equip.org/free/ DE233.htm (accessed 8 April 2004).

Owens, David C. "Books & Culture Corner: A Cry for Help." *Christianity Today,* 13 June 2002. http://www.christianity today.com/ct/2002/123/14.0.html (accessed 8 April 2004).

Southern Baptist Convention. *The Baptist Faith and Message.* Nashville: Southern Baptist Convention, 2000.

Woodward, Kenneth L. "The Bible and the Qur'an." *Newsweek* 11, February 2002: 51–57.

Chapter Eight—Rich Resources of the South

"Canadian Oil Company Orders Ethnic Cleansing in Sudan." *Abolish, the Anti-Slavery Portal,* 5 March 2002. http://www.i abolish.com/news/global/2002/talisman03-05-02.htm (accessed 8 April 2004).

"Famine in Sudan." *The New York Times,* 1998. http://www.ny times.com/library/world/africa/sudan-aid-list.html (accessed 8 April 2004).

"Oil in Sudan." *South Sudanese Friends International,* 25 June 2000. http://www.southsudanfriends.org/issues/oil000614 .html (accessed 8 April 2004).

"The Presbyterian Church of Sudan vs. Talisman Energy, Class Action Lawsuit." *Abolish, the Anti-Slavery Portal,* 2001. http://www.iabolish.com/classaction/default.htm (accessed 8 April 2004).

"The IRC in Sudan." *International Rescue Committee,* January 2002. http://www.theirc.org/index.cfm?section=where& locationID=40 (accessed 8 April 2004).

"The Scorched Earth: Oil and War in Sudan." *Christian Aid Media Report,* 2000. http://www.christian-aid.org.uk/indepth/0103suda/sudanoil.htm (accessed 8 April 2004).

"Statement by the President." *Office of the Press Secretary,* 21 October 2002. http://www.whitehouse.gov/news/releases/2002/10/20021021-10.html (accessed 8 April 2004).

"Sudan: Bush signs Peace Act." UN Office for the Coordination of Humanitarian Affairs. *Irin News,* 30 October 2002. http://www.irinnews.org/report.asp?ReportID=30540&SelectRegion=East_Africa&SelectCountry=SUDAN (accessed 8 April 2004).

"Sudan, Oil, Crimes Against Humanity . . . and Canada." *Urgent Action Bulletin,* 20 September 1999. http://www.sudan.activist.ca/info/uab1999sep20.html (accessed 8 April 2004).

"Sudan, The Harker Report." *Africa Policy Home Page.* http://www.africaaction.org/docs00/hark0002.htm (accessed 8 April 2004).

"Talisman Oil Advised, Further Abuses Could Result in Prosecution." *CorpWatch,* 2 May 2002. http://www.corpwatch.org/bulletins/PBD.jsp?articleid=2478 (accessed 8 April 2004).

"Sudan The Civilian Protection Monitoring Team." http://www.cpmtsudan.org/ (accessed 8 April 2004).

"Sudan: The Civilians Protection Monitoring Team." *U.S. Department of State,* 8 August 2003. http://www.state.gov/p/af/rls/fs/23132.htm (accessed 8 April 2004).

"Inter-Governmental Authority on Development." Nationmaster.com, 2003. http://www.nationmaster.com/kp/IGAD (accessed 8 April 2004).

Dwarkin, Anthony. "President Bush Signs Act to Promote Peace in

Sudan." *Crimes of War Project* 25, October 2002. http://www
.crimesofwar.org/onnews/news-sudan.html (accessed 9 April
2004).

Chapter Nine—Centuries of Slavery

Boucher, Richard. "Sudan Slavery Commission." *Washington Press
Release,* 25 March 2002. http://www.state.gov/r/pa/prs/ps/
2002/8906.htm (accessed 8 April 2004).

"Charities Who Buy Slaves Their Freedom May End Up Doing
Harm." *The Economist,* 7 February 2002. http://www.sudan
campaign.com/ (accessed 8 April 2004).

Davies, Karin. "Buying Freedom - $100.00 Each—for Sudan's
Slaves." *The Christian Science Monitor,* 13 February 1998.
http://www.csmonitor.com/durable/1998/02/13/intl/intl.3
.html (accessed 8 April 2004).

"Does Slavery Exist in Sudan." *Sudanese American Society,* 2 July
2001. http://www.sudan.net/news/press/postedr/38.shtml
(accessed 9 April 2004).

"Francis Bok Biographical Sketch." *Abolish, the Antislavery
Portal.* http://www.iabolish.com/news/press-kit/bio/francis
.htm (accessed 9 April 2004).

Hammond, Peter "The Forgotten Frontline—Sudan." *Frontline
Fellowship News,* 5 October 1995. http://www.visi.com/~home
lands//sudan/sudan_frontline.html (accessed 9 April 2004).

Niemeyer, Lucian. "The Sudan Slave Story." *Christian Solidarity
International,* December 2000. http://www.lnsart.com/Sudan
%20Slave%20Story.htm (accessed 9 April 2004).

"Operation Lifeline Sudan: The Work of UNICEF and The
World Food Program." *United Nations,* 2001. http://www

.un.org/av/photo/subjects/sudan.htm (accessed 9 April 2004).

Rather, Dan. "The Slave Trade." *60 Minutes* II, 15 May 2002. http://www.cbsnews.com/stories/2002/01/02/60II/main322 870.shtml (accessed 9 April 2004).

Reeves, Eric. "A UN Seat for Genocide." *The Washington Post,* 15 August 2000. Tuesday, Final Edition, section OP-ED: A23.

Reeves, Eric. "Rapacious Instincts in Sudan." *The Nation,* 4 June 2001.

"Ripping of the Slave 'Redeemers.'" *Washington Post,* 26 February 2002. http://www.sudancampaign.com/ (accessed 9 April 2004).

"Slave Raid in Sudan, Dozens Missing." *Sudan Divestment Campaign,* 19 June 2002. http://www.ga0.org/campaign/raid (accessed 9 April 2004).

"Slavery and Slave Redemption in the Sudan." *Human Rights News,* March 2002. http://www.hrw.org/backgrounder/africa/ sudanupdate.htm (accessed 9 April 2004).

"Slavery in Sudan, Did You Know?" *Mission S.U.D.A.N.* http://www.missionsudan.com/ (accessed 9 April 2004).

"Sudan Q & A." *The American Friends Service Committee.* http://www.members.aol.com/casmasalc/newpage8.htm (accessed 9 April 2004).

Taylor, Teresa. "Capital Market Sanctions Hold Key to Cessation of Atrocities and Peace in Good Faith by Khartoum." *Survivors Rights' International,* 10 September 2001. http://www.survivorsrightsinternational.org/sri_news/ press_release_spa.mv (accessed 9 April 2004).

"The Great Slave Scam." *Irish Times,* 23 February 2002. http://www.sudancampaign.com/ (accessed 9 April 2004).

"Turning a Profit on the Price of Freedom." *Pittsburg Post Gazette,* 1 March 2002. http://www.sudancampaign.com/ (accessed 9 April 2004).

Chapter Ten—Kakuma Today

EENET. "Life in Kakuma, Kenya." http://www.eenet.org.uk/ newsletters/news6/page11.shtml, (accessed 9 April 2004).

"High School Education for Sudanese Refugees in Kenya." *Episcopal Relief and Development,* 2002. http://www.er-d.org/ projectsforhope17.htm (accessed 9 April 2004).

Imhoff, Frank. "Focusing on the Future at Kakuma Refugee Camp in Kenya." *WorldwideFaith News,* 9 June 2001. http://www.wfn.org/2001/06/msg00076.html (accessed 9 April 2004).

Mburu, Evans. "Life in Kakuma, Kenya." *Enabling Education Network,* 5 October 2002. http://www.eenet.org.uk/news letters/news6/page11.shtml (accessed 9 April 2004).

Phillips, Jason. "Food Supplies Dwindle at Kakuma Refugee Camp; IRC Raises Concern in Washington," 4 June 2002. http://www.theirc.org/news/index.cfm?fa=newsdetail&news ID=905 (accessed 9 April 2004).

Lutheran World Federation. "Kakuma Refugee Camp." http://www .lwfkenyasudan.org/kakuma_refugee_camp.htm (accessed 9 April 2004).

Chapter Eleven—The Church in Kakuma and Sudan

"Important Dates in the History of the Church in Sudan." http://www.eglisesoudan.org/english/dates.htm (accessed 9 April 2004).

"Facts have Faces." *Church World Services,* 2002. http://www.church worldservice.org/FactsHaveFaces/sudanfs.html (accessed 9 April 2004).

"Reformed Witness in the Sudan." *Middle East Reformed Fellowship,* November 1999. http://www.gospelcom.net/woh/merf/articles/sudan1.html (accessed 9 April 2004).

"Sudan." *New Sudan Council of Churches* 2002. http://www .brethren.org/genbd/global_mission/Sudan/ (accessed 9 April 2004).

Chapter Twelve—America the Springboard

"7-Foot-7 Ex-NBA Player to Join Hockey Team." *Click 2 Houston,* 13 November 2002. http://www.click2houston.com/sh/sports/stories/sports-178374020021113-111107.html (accessed 9 April 2004).

Aid Sudan Foundation. http://www.aidsudan.org (accessed 9 April 2004).

Chisholm, Raymond N. "Rebuilding the Infrastructure of a War Torn Nation." *The Sudan,* 24 July 2002. http://www .chisholm.org/Sudan%20Congress.htm (accessed 9 April 2004).

Directors of Health Promotion and Education. "Guinea Worm Disease." http://www.astdhpphe.org/infect/guinea.html (accessed 9 April 2004).

Information Request:

If you would like additional information on how you can contribute financially or volunteer to help with the Lost Boys, visit www.aidsudan.org or complete the following and mail to:

Aid Sudan Foundation
P. O. Box 924176
Houston, Texas 77292

Name

_____

Address

_____

City_____State _____

Zip _____

E-mail

_____

I'm interested in: _____

_____

_____

_____